How Home Theater and HDTV Work

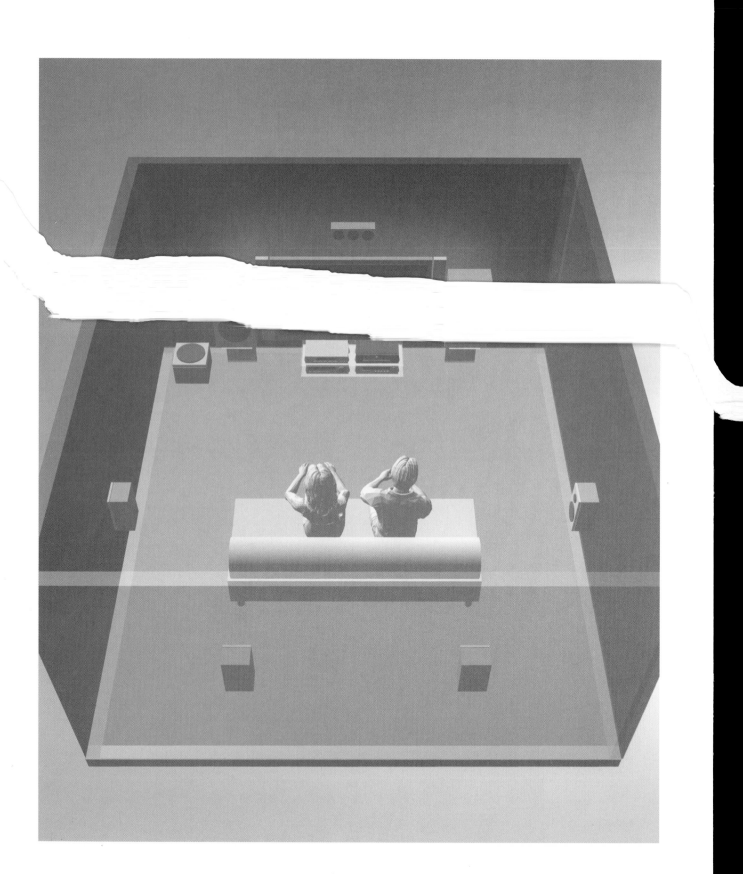

How Home Theater and HDTV Work

Michael Miller

Illustrations by Michael Troller

800 East 96th Street
Indianapolis, IN 46240 USA

How Home Theater and HDTV Work

Copyright © 2006 by Que Publishing

Associate Publisher	Greg Wiegand
Executive Editor	Rick Kughen
Development Editor	Todd Brakke
Managing Editor	Charlotte Clapp
Project Editor	Tonya Simpson
Production Editor	Megan Wade
Indexer	Aaron Black
Proofreader	Melinda Gutowski
Technical Editor	Thomas Mincy
Reviewers	Gareth Branwyn, Jordan Gold, and Thomas Mincy
Publishing Coordinator	Sharry Lee Gregory
Interior Designer	Anne Jones
Cover Designers	Michael Troller and Anne Jones
Page Layout	Michelle Mitchell

International Standard Book Number: 0-7897-3445-1

Library of Congress Catalog Card Number: 2005925005

Printed in the United States of America

First Printing: November 2005

08 07 06 05   4 3 2 1

Trademarks

Warning and Disclaimer

Bulk Sales

Que Publishing offers excellent discounts on this book when ordered in quantity for bulk purchases or special sales. For more information, please contact

U.S. Corporate and Government Sales

1-800-382-3419

corpsales@pearsontechgroup.com

For sales outside the United States, please contact

International Sales

international@pearsoned.com

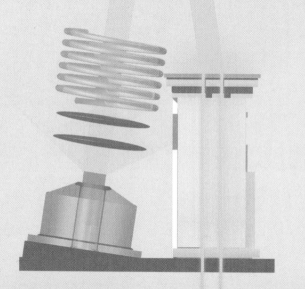

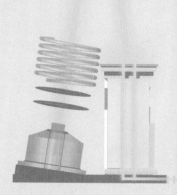

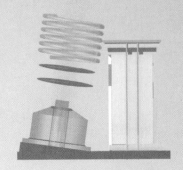

DAC

MICHAEL MILLER has authored more than 60 best-selling books over the past 15 years, including *Absolute Beginner's Guide to Computer Basics*, *Absolute Beginner's Guide to eBay*, and *The Complete Idiot's Guide to Home Theater Systems*. Mr. Miller has established a reputation for clearly explaining technical topics to nontechnical readers and for offering useful, real-world advice about complicated topics. More information can be found at the author's website, located at www.molehillgroup.com.

MICHAEL TROLLER got his start in the fields of communication and design by drawing *Peanuts* characters on his assignments in the second grade (with thanks to an unusually perceptive and kind-hearted teacher, Mrs. Nolke, who just kept giving him more paper). So many decades on from this humble and humorous start, Michael continues to create effective and engaging art in multiple media. Michael Troller Design is located in the San Francisco Bay Area and works for clients large and small, near and far to realize their dreams and potential. Michael has illustrated two previous books in this series: *How Networks Work* and *How the Internet Works*.

Michael Miller would like to thank the usual suspects at Que, including but not limited to Rick Kughen, Greg Wiegand, Todd Brakke, Megan Wade, Tonya Simpson, and Thomas Mincy. My special thanks go to Michael Troller, who supplied the amazingly detailed and beautiful illustrations that make this book what it is.

Michael Troller would like to thank his indulgent parents, John and Elizabeth; his even more indulgent wife, Noël; and his greatest source of strength and inspiration, his two marvelous sons, Lukas and John Duncan.

As the reader of this book, *you* are our most important critic and commentator. We value your opinion and want to know what we're doing right, what we could do better, what areas you'd like to see us publish in, and any other words of wisdom you're willing to pass our way.

As an executive editor for Que, I welcome your comments. You can email or write me directly to let me know what you did or didn't like about this book—as well as what we can do to make our books better.

Please note that I cannot help you with technical problems related to the topic of this book. We do have a User Services group, however, where I will forward specific technical questions related to the book.

When you write, please be sure to include this book's title and author as well as your name, email address, and phone number. I will carefully review your comments and share them with the author and editors who worked on the book.

Email: feedback@quepublishing.com

Mail: Rick Kughen
Executive Editor
Que Publishing
800 East 96th Street
Indianapolis, IN 46240 USA

For more information about this book or another Que Publishing title, visit our website at www.quepublishing.com. Type the ISBN (excluding hyphens) or the title of a book in the Search field to find the page you're looking for.

Big-time entertainment used to be something you went out for. When you wanted to watch big-screen spectacle, you headed to the local movie theater. When you wanted to listen to great music, you headed out to a live concert. Entertainment in the home was limited to viewing sitcoms on a small-screen TV, or listening to the top-forty hits on the radio.

That's all different now, thanks to the advent of home theater systems and the coming of high-definition television. Now the big screen is in the living room, projecting images larger than life and twice as sharp. Musical choices are limitless and reproduced with digital fidelity. With so many first-class entertainment choices available, why leave home at all?

When it comes to assembling your own home entertainment system, the choices are equally limitless, to the point of being a little intimidating. You want a big TV, but what kind should you get—the old-fashioned picture-tube kind, a fancy rear projector, or one of those cool flat-screen models? What do you need to get high-definition television? How many speakers do you need, and where should they go? And all those acronyms—DLP, LCD, HDTV, DTS, DBS, and on and on and on—what do they mean? The technology is exciting, but it's also confusing.

That's where this book comes in. *How Home Theater and HDTV Work* introduces you to all the technologies used in today's home entertainment systems, but in a way that's easy to understand. You'll not only read about how these technologies work, but you'll *see* how they work, thanks to the detailed, yet user-friendly, illustrations within. Want to know the difference between regular television and high-definition TV? How about how to configure your living room for surround sound? Well, this book will *show* you everything you want to know, visually. It's a great way to learn about all these exciting developments.

To make it easier to find what you're interested in, this book is divided into 22 separate chapters, organized into six major sections. It's easy to go directly to any given topic; you can skip around as you like, or read the book from front to back, whichever works best for you.

Part I, "How Television Works," provides a general introduction to the medium we all know and love. You'll see how traditional broadcast TV works, from the television studio to your home, as well as how cable and satellite broadcasts are transmitted and received.

Part II, "How High-Definition Television Works," examines the new HDTV technology. You'll see how HDTV broadcasts differ from standard television, how digital TV differs from older analog broadcasts, and how the various screen aspect ratios work. You'll even learn about letterboxing widescreen movies, and how normal programming is displayed on a widescreen TV.

Part III, "How Video Displays Work," is all about the screen. You'll learn about CRT displays, rear projection displays, front projection displays, and the new flat panel displays. You'll see all the various technologies involved, from DLP to LCD to plasma; discover how the different displays compare; and find out how to choose the best display for your own home theater system.

Part IV, "How Audio Works," introduces the audio aspect of an audio/video system. This section is all about speakers and receivers and power amplifiers; this is also where you'll learn about the various types of surround sound systems, including both Dolby Digital and DTS.

Part V, "How Audio/Video Sources Work," is about the equipment that provides your home entertainment. You'll see how all these components work, including videotape players, DVD players, and the new hard-disk digital video recorders. You'll even learn how to play digital music via a digital media server or media center PC.

Finally, Part VI, "How Home Theater Systems Work," shows you how all of these components fit together. You'll see how to set up your own home theater system, learn which video and audio cables to use, and discover how to operate everything from a single universal remote control.

By the time you're done reading this book, you'll know how all these wonderful audio/video components work, and be ready to put together your own home theater system. Trust me—after you've watched a high-definition movie in your living room, complete with surround sound effects, you'll never go back to a plain old television set. Home theater and HDTV are the future of entertainment—and *How Home Theater and HDTV Work* will help you prepare for that future, today.

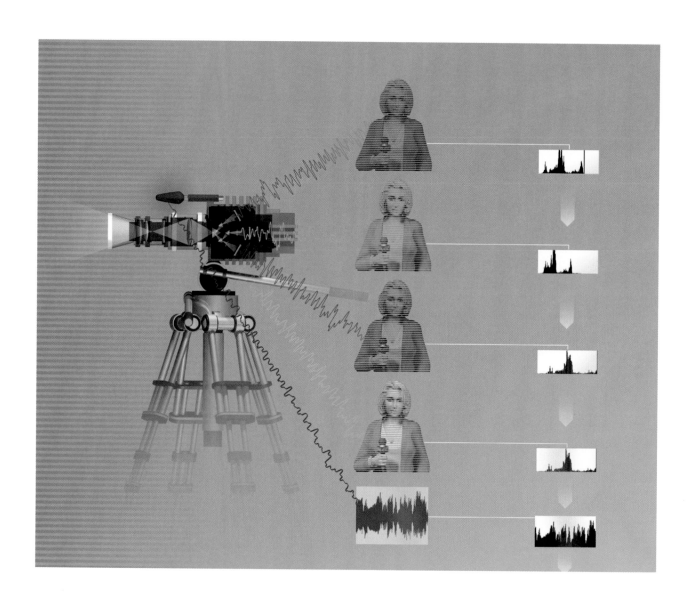

P A R T

HOW TELEVISION WORKS

THE centerpiece of any home theater system is the television set. Television technology has been around for more than 75 years, evolving from black and white to color, from tube-type construction to solid state design, from analog transmission to digital transmission, and from fuzzy standard definition signals to crystal clear high definition broadcasts. Television has come a long way from the 10" monochrome sets of the 1950s to the 60" HDTV sets of today.

Most of us can't remember a time without television. From the cartoons of our youth to the miniseries and movies that make up today's broadcast schedule, television has been our window to the world around us, both reflecting and shaping our society in subtle and not-so-subtle ways. Our memories of major events are memories of watching those events on television—the Kennedy assassination, the Apollo 11 moon landing, the 9/11 attacks. Television informs us, entertains us, and comforts us.

Television technology was first demonstrated in 1926, when John Logie Baird showed a crude mechanical television apparatus to members of the Royal Institution in London. In the United States, Bell Telephone Labs and AT&T demonstrated television broadcasting in 1927, sending pictures and sound (by wire) from Washington, DC, to New York City. Other companies were also working on the technology, chief among them General Electric and RCA.

The first public television broadcasts occurred in 1928, on New York station WRGB. By 1937 there were eighteen experimental television stations operating in the United States, and commercial television broadcasting began three years later. Television really took off after World War II; by 1950 there were close to 10 million sets in use in the United States, and this number mushroomed to more than 70 million sets by 1960.

Local programming gave way to network programming in the 1950s, following the model established by network radio. NBC, CBS, ABC, and DuMont were the main networks back then; their network stations broadcast almost exclusively on VHF channels 2-13. DuMont would fall by the wayside by 1955, leaving in place the three-network system that would hold (with the addition of the Public Broadcasting System) until the 1980s. From the mid-1950s onward, independent stations tended to be relegated to the less-popular UHF channels.

Everything was in black and white through the 1940s, 1950s, and mid-1960s. That was when color broadcasts became common, thanks to new color television sets by RCA and a "living color" push by NBC. The other manufacturers and networks followed suit, and by the end of the decade all the networks' schedules consisted entirely of color programming.

Television was almost exclusively *broadcast* television until the early 1970s, dominated by the three major networks—ABC, CBS, and NBC—broadcasting over-the-air via thousands of local stations. While transmission via cable had long been a necessity in rural areas (due to poor over-the-air reception), cable didn't become a national factor until 1972, when pay service HBO was introduced to cable systems across the country. Today the majority of Americans receive their television signals either via cable or via satellite, with more than a hundred different channels available.

More than two-thirds of U.S. households receive cable television. In most instances, cable offers a clearer, more reliable picture than over-the-air broadcasts, as well as literally hundreds of programming choices. The cable set-top box (STB) has become ubiquitous in the American living room, along with the requisite universal remote control unit. Of course, a lot of cable choices are available, beyond the simple question of whether to subscribe to HBO and other premium services; most cable subscribers have a choice of analog or digital service, as well as a basic STB or one with a built-in digital video recorder.

Those households that don't have cable often have satellite television service instead. The two competing American satellite services (DIRECTV and Dish Network) offer roughly the same amount and types of programming offered by the cable companies, but their signals are sent via orbiting satellites rather than underground coaxial cable. The satellite services offer all-digital programming, which is an advantage over the part-analog, part-digital service offered by most cable companies—even if the service sometimes goes out during a heavy rainstorm or is blocked by tall trees and buildings. (There has to be a clear line-of-sight between the satellite dish on your roof and the satellite orbiting overhead.)

So, broadcast television remains a mainstay in living rooms across the country, although the television tuner is now supplemented by the DVD player and hard disk recorder. Many of today's television broadcasts feature surround sound, widescreen aspect ratios, and (where available) high definition pictures. The quality of television technology has improved just as the quantity of available stations has increased.

Tomorrow's televisions will be bigger, wider, and sharper, but they'll still be based on the same basic transmission technology first introduced seventy-five years ago. Television signals will still be broadcast via a transmitter of some sort (or fed through a cable), and received by a tuner built into or sitting on top of a television display. Tomorrow's signals are likely to be digital instead of analog, however, with much higher resolution and better sound. And it's likely that the concept of a regular network schedule will be abandoned in favor of programming on demand, supplemented by the "watch it when you want" time-shifting enabled by hard disk video recorders.

No matter what new sources of entertainment might be introduced in the coming years, we'll still be watching our television. And whether the star of the hour is Lucille Ball, Johnny Carson, Jerry Seinfeld, or some new discovery, we'll continue to dim the lights, lean back on the living couch, grab the popcorn, and enjoy the show.

CHAPTER

1

How Broadcast Television Works

FOR years we've received our television programming over the air, broadcast from a local television station and received by a set-top or roof-top antenna attached to the living room TV set. While there are now plenty of other ways to receive audio/video programming—via cable, satellite, and DVD—many Americans still receive over-the-air (OTA) broadcasts, and the OTA broadcast system is the basis of all the other transmission systems that have developed since then.

There are several technological principles on which OTA television broadcasts are based. First of these is the science of perception. What we perceive as a moving picture is actually a series of still pictures, flashed one after another in rapid succession. The pictures flash by so quickly that this succession of pictures flow together and appear to be in movement.

This perceived motion is even more extraordinary when you consider that each individual picture is actually comprised of hundreds of individual horizontal lines, painted across the screen one after another. That's how the picture is encoded for transmission; the original picture is sliced into these horizontal lines and then the horizontal lines are redisplayed at the receiving end of the chain. Your mind combines these lines and "sees" a complete picture—one full picture every 1/30 of a second.

Finally, we're faced with the challenge of transmitting all those lines and pictures from the local television station to your house. This is accomplished using radio waves, which travel through the air from the transmitting antenna to the receiving antenna. Every television station broadcasts at a specific frequency in either the Very High Frequency (VHF) or Ultra High Frequency (UHF) band. For example, television channel 8 is assigned to VHF frequency 181.25MHz; channel 40 is assigned to UHF frequency 627.25MHz.

At that assigned frequency, the television station broadcasts a signal that is exactly 6MHz wide. Within this 6MHz bandwidth is all the information necessary to create the moving pictures and sound of a television program. Part of that 6MHz signal is devoted to the basic black-and-white component of the picture; another part of the signal is devoted to the color component; and yet another part of the signal is devoted to the audio component. Put them all together, and you have the television signal your home antenna receives and your TV set displays. It might sound complex, but it works!

How the Traditional Broadcast Television System Works

Transmission tower

1 While early experimental televisions used various mechanical systems to reproduce picture and sound, all modern televisions are electronic in nature. It doesn't matter whether you're watching a older CRT-type television or a newer plasma or projection model, the way the electronic signal becomes a picture on your set is the same all across the United States.

Modulator

3 The picture and sound information is encoded onto a 6MHz signal, which is sent via satellite (or, in some instances, on tape) from the television network headquarters to the local broadcasting stations.

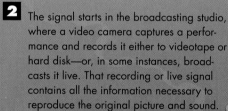

Video camera

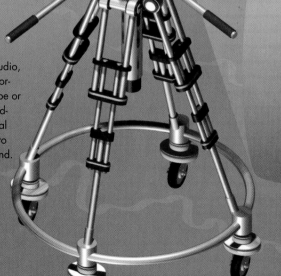

2 The signal starts in the broadcasting studio, where a video camera captures a performance and records it either to videotape or hard disk—or, in some instances, broadcasts it live. That recording or live signal contains all the information necessary to reproduce the original picture and sound.

Subject is divided into horizontal scan lines.

6MHz signal

Even number interlaced scan lines

Odd number interlaced scan lines

4 Each local station then amplifies the encoded signal and broadcasts it from a transmitting antenna. The signals from the antenna travel through the air until they're received by a receiving antenna connected to your television set. The antenna is connected to your set's tuner, which separates out the signals by broadcast frequency; it's the tuner that identifies a signal at a given frequency as being channel 3 or 4 or 65.

5 Once received, the electronic signal is now decoded into its component parts. The sound signal is sent to your television's audio amplifier, and the picture signal is sent through various video processing circuits.

6 The decoded and processed video signal is separated into a series of horizontal lines, which are flashed sequentially onto your display device. In the American NTSC system, there are 525 of these horizontal lines, separated into even-numbered and odd-numbered lines that are traced on the screen in separate passes; the two sets of lines combine to form a complete interlaced picture. Thirty of these complete 525-line pictures are painted onto your screen every second.

Audio amplifier

TV with antenna

7 As this succession of discrete images flashes before your eyes, your mind fills in the gaps and "sees" a seamless moving picture. Thus, your television set reproduces what was originally recorded by the video camera—via an entirely electronic process.

How Electronic Television Systems Work

1 The image seen by a video camera is divided into a series of horizontal (left to right) scan lines in an electronic signal. This electronic signal contains both black-and-white (*luminance*) and color (*chrominance*) information, as well as audio information.

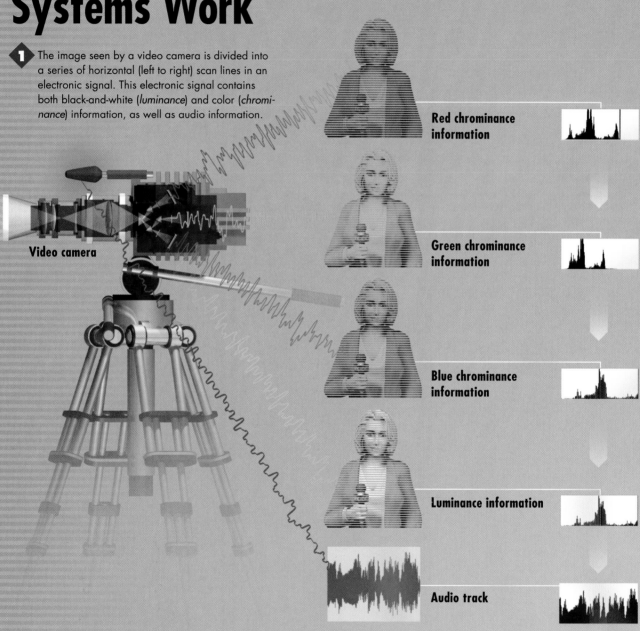

Video camera

Red chrominance information

Green chrominance information

Blue chrominance information

Luminance information

Audio track

2 The electronic signal is modulated into a 6MHz radio frequency signal and then transmitted from the broadcast source to your television receiver.

Modulator

Odd numbered scan lines		Even numbered scan lines
	449	448
	451	450
	453	452
	455	454
	457	456
	459	458
	461	460
	463	462
	465	464
	467	466
	469	468
	471	470
	473	472
	475	474
	477	476
	479	478
		480

3 The modulated signal is decoded by your television receiver and sent to your display device.

4 An American standard definition picture (NTSC system) is painted on the display via a series of horizontal scan lines. There are 525 total scan lines, 480 of which transmit picture information. These 480 lines are divided into even-numbered and odd-numbered *fields*. Each line is painted on the display from left to right, and the lines of each field from top to bottom.

Scan line 1

Scan line 2

479

480

Odd number interlaced scan lines

Even number interlaced scan lines

5 When one field is complete, the second field is then painted; the two alternating fields are *interlaced* to create one complete frame of a moving picture.

6 When one frame is complete, the two fields of the next frame are then painted on the display. Thirty frames per second are painted, which creates the appearance of a continuously moving picture.

How Television Signals Are Transmitted

Transmitting tower antenna

6MHz radio waves

1 After a television signal has been encoded electronically at the source, it is sent to a powerful transmitting antenna for broadcast. This antenna amplifies the signal so that it can travel long distances.

Video input

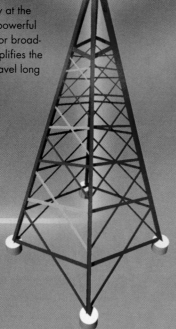

2 The television signal is a radio wave in the VHF *(Very High Frequency)* or UHF *(ultra high freqency)* band that travels in a straight line. To receive a television signal, you must be in a direct line of sight to the transmitting antenna, within the so-called "radio horizon." This radio horizon is actually about a third farther than the natural horizon, due to the refractive nature of radio waves. While small obstacles such as trees or small buildings typically don't block the entire signal, a larger obstacle—such as a large building or a mountain—can reflect or distort the radio waves.

Direct path

Reflected signal

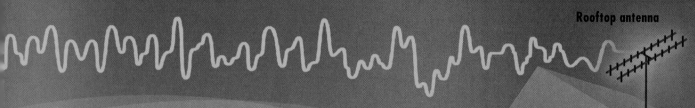

Rooftop antenna

3 The television signal is received by a receiving antenna or aerial connected to a television set (also called a *television receiver*). This can be a large, external antenna mounted on your roof or a smaller set of "rabbit ears" attached directly to your television set. Any reflections or distortions are seen as ghosts of the original signal.

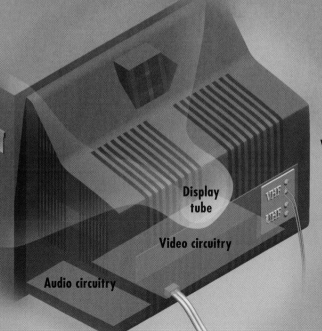

Display tube

VHF
VHF

Video circuitry

Audio circuitry

VHF antenna connection

4 The received signal is sent to the tuner section of the television receiver. The tuner adjusts to the frequency of each individual channel and then sends that signal to the receiver's audio and video processing circuitry.

How Television Frequencies Work

1 Every standard definition television signal takes up a total of 6MHz of bandwidth. Different parts of that 6MHz bandwidth are devoted to different parts of the television signal.

2 At one end of the 6MHz signal is a vestigial sideband (VSB) that provides a 1.25MHz guard band between the video carrier and the bottom frequency in the channel. The VSB is used to reduce interference between adjoining channels.

Picture carrier

Vestigal sideband

1.25MHz

3 The picture signal is divided into black-and-white and color components. The picture carrier signal for black-and-white information is located at 1.25MHz.

6 MHz

Color subcarrier

Sound carrier

0.25MHz guard band

5 The carrier signal for sound information is located 4.5MHz above the picture carrier.

6 An additional 0.25MHz guard band exists at the high end of the signal to provide further buffer against adjacent-channel interference.

4.83MHz

5.75MHz

6MHz

4 The chrominance subcarrier signal for color information is located 3.58MHz above the picture carrier. A phase shift in the chrominance signal determines which color to display; the amplitude of the signal determines the saturation.

How Television Signals Work

The electromagnetic spectrum

Infrared

Frequency

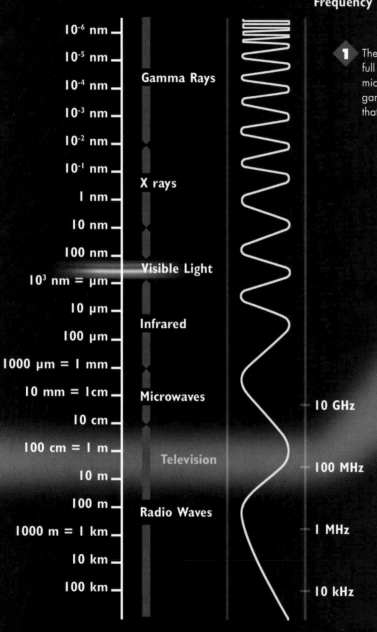

10^{-6} nm	
10^{-5} nm	
10^{-4} nm	Gamma Rays
10^{-3} nm	
10^{-2} nm	
10^{-1} nm	
1 nm	X rays
10 nm	
100 nm	
10^3 nm = μm	Visible Light
10 μm	
100 μm	Infrared
1000 μm = 1 mm	
10 mm = 1cm	Microwaves
10 cm	
100 cm = 1 m	Television
10 m	
100 m	Radio Waves
1000 m = 1 km	
10 km	
100 km	

10 GHz

100 MHz

1 MHz

10 kHz

1 The electromagnetic spectrum contains the full range of radiation from radio waves and microwaves through visible light, X-rays, and gamma rays. This radiation is simply energy that expands as it travels.

2 Radio waves occupy a very small part of the electromagnetic spectrum, from approximately 10 kilohertz (KHz) to 10 gigahertz (GHz). Different frequencies within this segment are devoted to different types of broadcasting. For example, AM radio signals are located between 535KHz and 1.7 megahertz (MHz), and shortwave radio signals are located between 5.8MHz and 26.1MHz.

Microwave, Radar, Satellite

Television   FM Radio

AM Radio

Power, Telephone

Frequency

EHF

SHF — 10 GHz

UHF

VHF — 100 MHz

HF

MF — 1 MHz

LF

VLF — 10 kHz

VF

ELF

3 Broadcast television signals are assigned to four different portions of the spectrum. Channels 2–4 are assigned to the VHF-Lo band between 54MHz and 72MHz, while channels 5 and 6 are assigned to the VHF-Lo band between 76MHz and 88MHz. There is a short gap in the spectrum for FM radio signals; then television channels 7–13 are assigned to the VHF-Hi band between 174MHz and 216MHz. The upper channels (14–68) are assigned to the UHF (ultrahigh frequency) band between 470MHz and 854MHz.

North American Television Channel Frequencies

Channel	Band	Frequency
14-68	UHF	470MHz-854MHz
7-13	VHF-Hi	174MHz-216MHz
5-6	VHF-Lo	76MHz-88MHz
2-4	VHF-Lo	54MHz-72MHz

How Resolution Is Measured

1 The sharpness of a television signal is reflected by the signal's resolution, measured in terms of vertical and horizontal lines of resolution. This measurement can be made with the standard television test pattern, shown here. The resolution is determined by many alternating light and dark lines that can be distinguished from one another when spaced close together. When the lines start to blur together, the resolution limit has been exceeded. The more lines of resolution, the sharper the picture.

Black-and-white test pattern

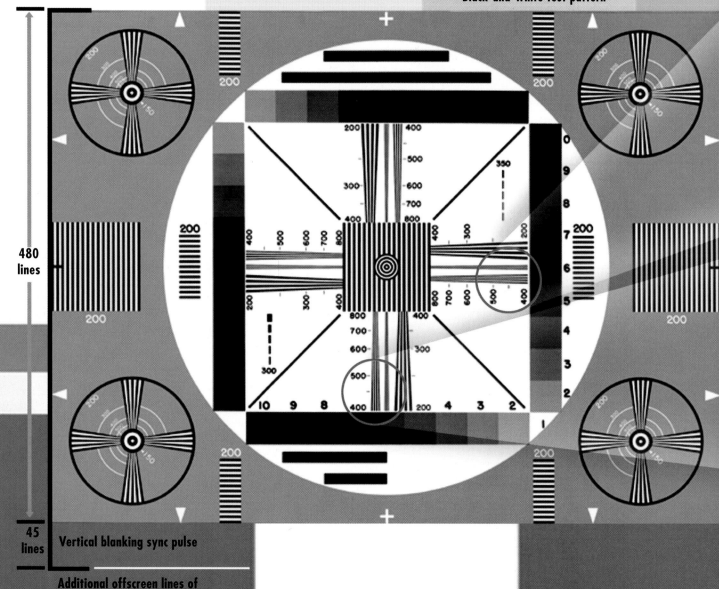

480 lines

45 lines

Vertical blanking sync pulse

Additional offscreen lines of television signal information

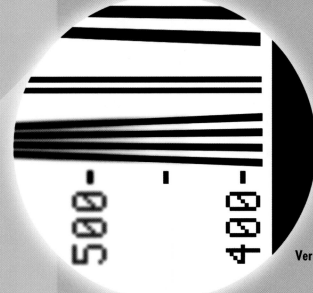

2 *Vertical resolution* refers to the lines that are scanned horizontally (from left to right) but are counted vertically (top to bottom), like the slats on a Venetian blind. The vertical resolution of a picture is set by the transmission system or format. This number is static and doesn't change from set to set within a given system. In the standard definition NTSC system, there are 480 lines of vertical resolution; in the European PAL system, there are 576 lines of vertical resolution; in the 780p high-definition system, there are 780 lines of vertical resolution; and in the 1080i high-definition system, there are 1,080 lines of vertical resolution.

Vertical line test pattern

3 *Horizontal resolution* refers to the lines or columns that run vertically but are counted horizontally across the width of the screen. This number varies by the source of the transmission and by the quality of the receiving unit and display. For example, the horizontal resolution is VHS tape is about 240 lines, standard definition broadcast TV is about 330 lines, laserdisc is about 400 lines, and DVD is 480 lines. (All measurements are for 4:3 aspect NTSC formats.)

Horizontal line test pattern

Wasted Lines
In the NTSC system, we don't see all 525 horizontal scan lines. Of the total number of lines available, 45 are black; these contain the sync pulse for the video signal. Only 480 scan lines are actually seen on the screen, thus resulting in a vertical resolution of 480 lines.

How the NTSC, PAL, and SECAM Systems Compare

American television viewers might be surprised to learn that the television they watch in the United States isn't the same as that shown in many other countries. That's because three different SDTV color broadcast standards are currently in use around the globe. The American National Television System Committee (NTSC) system was the first standard adopted, in 1953, and as such isn't quite as technically advanced as systems developed more recently. The Phase Alternation by Line (PAL) system was developed in the U.K. and Germany, while the Systeme électronique Colour avec Memoire (SECAM) system was developed in France. Because both these European systems use a larger number of scan lines, they are incompatible with the American NTSC system; you can't play NTSC discs and tapes on a PAL or SECAM television, and vice versa.

Fortunately, the global community has adopted a single worldwide standard for digital HDTV broadcasts, one that can work with the various electrical voltages used in different countries. (This follows an aborted Japanese attempt to introduce an analog HDTV system.) So, HDTV programming can be shown in any country around the world, with no expensive conversion required.

NTSC vs. PAL vs. SECAM

System	Full Name	Developing Countries	First Color Broadcast	Total Scan Lines	Vertical Resolution	Aspect Ratio	Frame Rate (frames per second)
NTSC	National Television System Committee	United States	1953	525	480	4:3	30
PAL	Phase Alternation by Line	United Kingdom Germany	1967	625	576	4:3	25
SECAM	Systeme électronique Couleur avec Memoire	France	1967	625	576	4:3	25

Different Systems

Color broadcasting technology was adopted at different times in different countries. The United States was first with color television, adopting the 525-line NTSC standard in 1953. Europe was slower to move from black and white to color and adopted two more-advanced technologies: PAL and SECAM, both 625-line systems. Most critics agree that the earlier NTSC system is inferior to the later PAL and SECAM systems, especially in terms of accurate and consistent color reproduction.

CHAPTER

2

How Cable Television Works

CABLE television was first developed for entirely practical reasons. Many rural viewers were located too far away from the big-city transmitting antennas and couldn't receive the signals of many (if any) major television stations. Cable was used to transmit these far-away television stations to rural customers.

The first cable network was established in 1948, when remote Pennsylvanians solved their reception problems by putting antennas on hills and running cables to their houses in the valleys. In the 1950s, rural cable systems began using microwave transmitting and receiving towers to capture even more distant signals. This made television available to people who lived outside the range of standard broadcasts—and, in some instances, gave cable customers access to several broadcast stations of the same national network.

By the early 1970s, many cable operators began offering additional channels, obtained from satellite broadcasters. Some of these channels, such as Atlanta's WTBS and Chicago's WGN, were simply local channels from elsewhere in the country. Other, more targeted, channels were developed specifically for the cable market. These new cable channels included the Cable News Network (CNN) and Home Box Office (HBO), the latter of which was the first "pay" channel.

Today, cable systems deliver hundreds of channels to more than 60 million American homes. Cable service is typically offered in differently priced *tiers*: The basic tier typically offers local stations, while subsequent tiers offer more focused programming and various pay channels. Many cable companies also offer on-demand programming, which enables the viewer to order up a menu of movies and other programs for a one-time viewing fee.

Whereas normal broadcast television signals travel through the air at a speed very close to the speed of light, cable signals are transmitted over a coaxial cable at about two thirds the speed of light. Newer cable systems transmit over longer distances via fiber-optic cable, and many cable services use encoded digital signals that let them offer more channels over the same bandwidth. Early cable systems operated with 200MHz of bandwidth, which enabled the transmission of just 33 channels. Today's systems use up to 550MHz of bandwidth, which—combined with digital encoding—enables the transmission of hundreds of channels.

How a Traditional Cable System Works

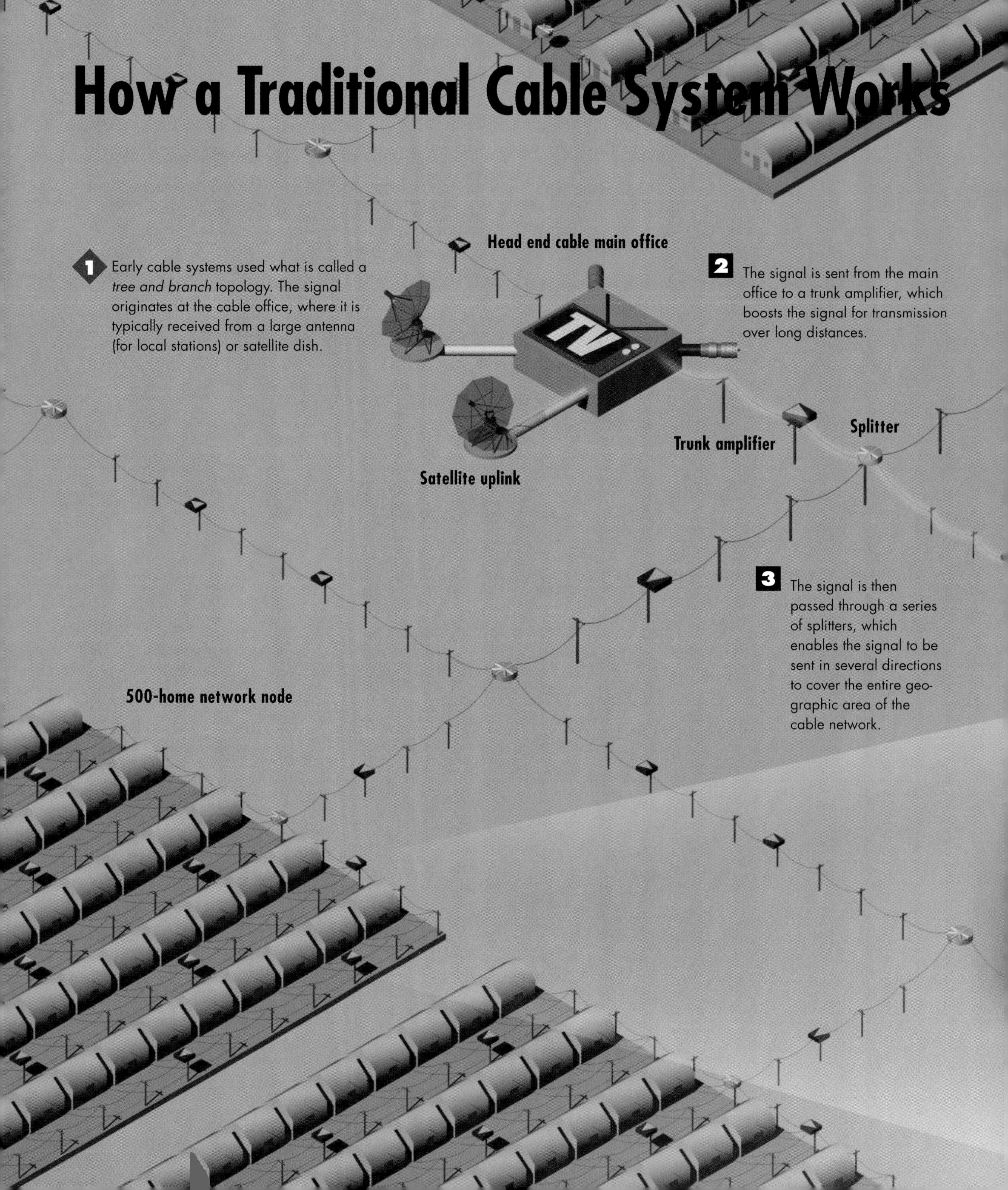

Head end cable main office

1 Early cable systems used what is called a *tree and branch* topology. The signal originates at the cable office, where it is typically received from a large antenna (for local stations) or satellite dish.

2 The signal is sent from the main office to a trunk amplifier, which boosts the signal for transmission over long distances.

Trunk amplifier

Splitter

Satellite uplink

3 The signal is then passed through a series of splitters, which enables the signal to be sent in several directions to cover the entire geographic area of the cable network.

500-home network node

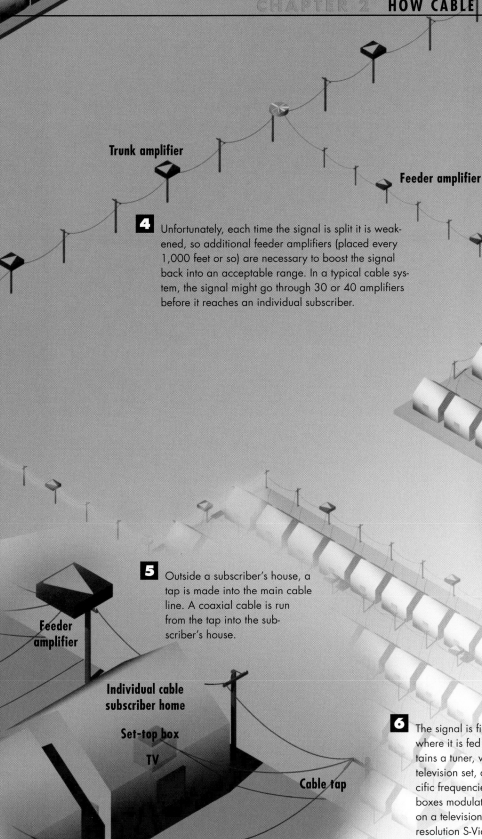

Trunk amplifier

Feeder amplifier

4 Unfortunately, each time the signal is split it is weakened, so additional feeder amplifiers (placed every 1,000 feet or so) are necessary to boost the signal back into an acceptable range. In a typical cable system, the signal might go through 30 or 40 amplifiers before it reaches an individual subscriber.

Feeder amplifier

5 Outside a subscriber's house, a tap is made into the main cable line. A coaxial cable is run from the tap into the subscriber's house.

Individual cable subscriber home

Set-top box

TV

Cable tap

6 The signal is finally received at the subscriber's house, where it is fed into the cable set-top box. This box contains a tuner, which functions like the tuner in a traditional television set, although it is customized to receive the specific frequencies used by the cable system. Most set-top boxes modulate the output signal to feed into channel 3 on a television receiver; newer boxes also offer higher-resolution S-Video and component video connections.

How a Fiber-optic Cable System Works

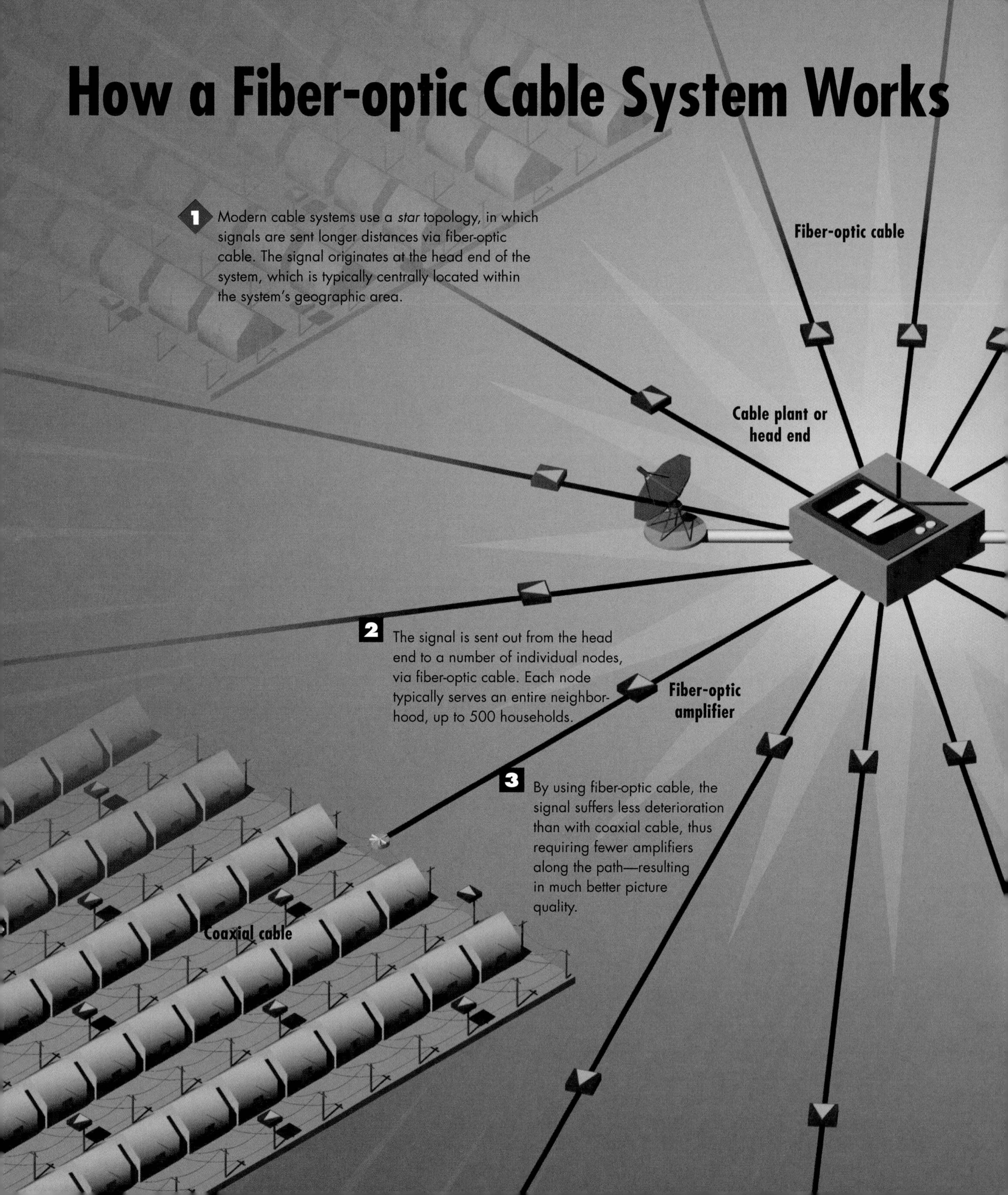

1 Modern cable systems use a *star* topology, in which signals are sent longer distances via fiber-optic cable. The signal originates at the head end of the system, which is typically centrally located within the system's geographic area.

Fiber-optic cable

Cable plant or head end

2 The signal is sent out from the head end to a number of individual nodes, via fiber-optic cable. Each node typically serves an entire neighborhood, up to 500 households.

Fiber-optic amplifier

3 By using fiber-optic cable, the signal suffers less deterioration than with coaxial cable, thus requiring fewer amplifiers along the path—resulting in much better picture quality.

Coaxial cable

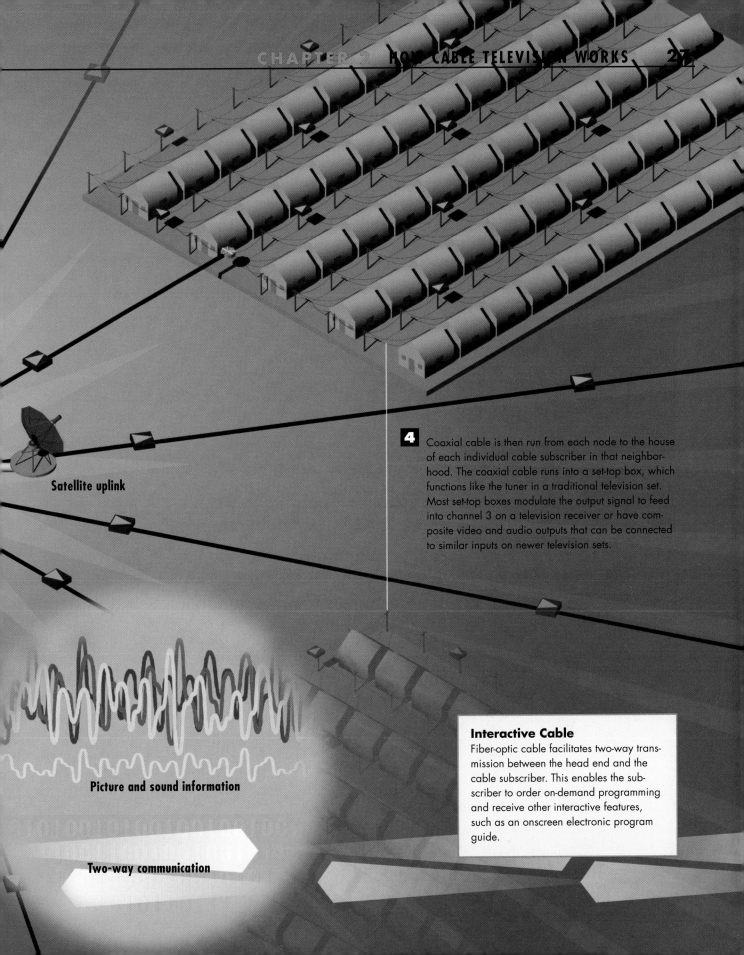

Satellite uplink

4 Coaxial cable is then run from each node to the house of each individual cable subscriber in that neighborhood. The coaxial cable runs into a set-top box, which functions like the tuner in a traditional television set. Most set-top boxes modulate the output signal to feed into channel 3 on a television receiver or have composite video and audio outputs that can be connected to similar inputs on newer television sets.

Picture and sound information

Two-way communication

Interactive Cable
Fiber-optic cable facilitates two-way transmission between the head end and the cable subscriber. This enables the subscriber to order on-demand programming and receive other interactive features, such as an onscreen electronic program guide.

How Digital Cable Works

Analog signals

Chrominance

Luminosity

Analog sound

1 Analog cable systems transmit signals via the same method used in broadcast television. Digital cable systems convert analog signals into digital signals, which take up less bandwidth and enable the cable company to offer more channels of programming.

Analog signals are digitized and compressed spatially and temporally.

Digitized picture

2 The digital signal is then subjected to MPEG-2 compression, which squeezes unnecessary bits of data out of the signal. For example, parts of a picture that aren't moving—that stay the same from frame to frame—don't have to be repeated; extracting this information lets the cable company put more information into the available bandwidth. This type of compression enables a cable company to fit 10 digital channels into the 6MHz bandwidth of a traditional analog channel.

A single analog signal fits in a 6MHz channel.

Using compression, digital cable systems can fit more channels in the same bandwidth.

Encoded frame

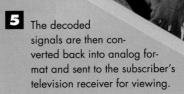

Set-top box

TV

4 When the signal is received by the subscriber's set-top box, those channels the subscriber has paid for are automatically decoded and uncompressed. Channels not subscribed to are not decoded, so they're not viewable.

5 The decoded signals are then converted back into analog format and sent to the subscriber's television receiver for viewing.

3 The digital signal is then encoded in a specific fashion, so that it is unreadable without first decoding it.

Encoding Versus Scrambling

On digital cable systems, unsubscribed-to channels are simply not decoded by the set-top box. On analog cable systems, unsubscribed-to channels have to be scrambled at the head end and then unscrambled by the set-top box.

Intraframe compression groups together similar colors within a single frame.

Intraframe compression compares multiple frames and records only changes.

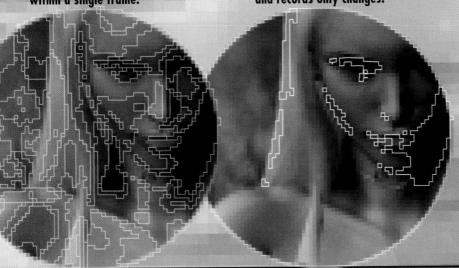

How On-Demand Cable Works

Powerful media servers

1 The interactivity of digital cable facilitates the reception of on-demand programming, enabling subscribers to order specific movies and programs and view them immediately after the request. It all starts with a network server at the cable system's head end, where available programming is stored on large hard disks.

High-performance hard disk arrays

Make a selection:
- Art
- Comedy
- Documentary
- Drama
- Science
more

Request spaceflight documentary.

2 When the subscriber orders an on-demand program, the request is sent upstream to the cable company's head end.

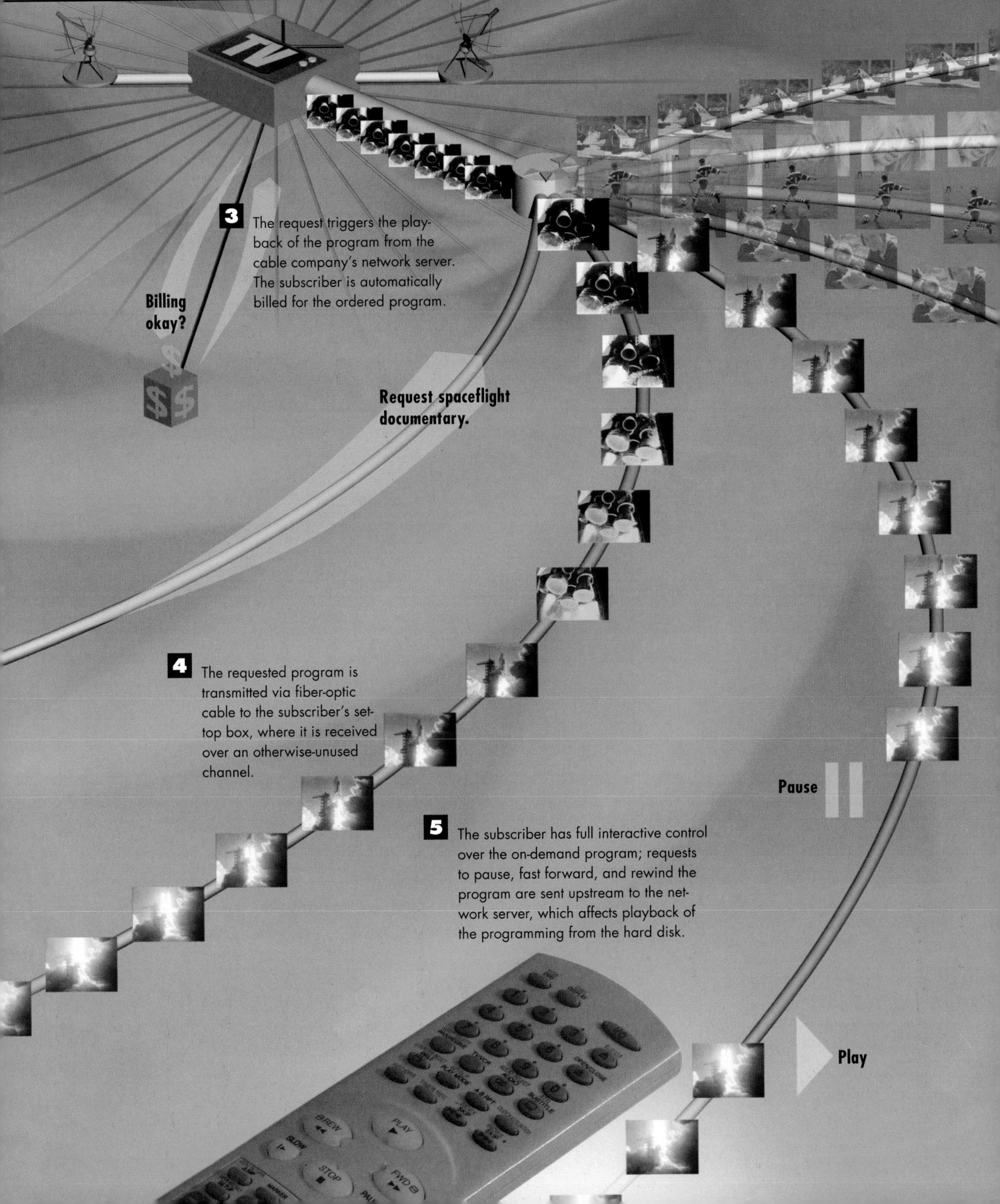

3 The request triggers the play-back of the program from the cable company's network server. The subscriber is automatically billed for the ordered program.

Billing okay?

Request spaceflight documentary.

4 The requested program is transmitted via fiber-optic cable to the subscriber's set-top box, where it is received over an otherwise-unused channel.

5 The subscriber has full interactive control over the on-demand program; requests to pause, fast forward, and rewind the program are sent upstream to the net-work server, which affects playback of the programming from the hard disk.

Pause

Play

CHAPTER

3

How Satellite Television Works

CONSUMER satellite television initially was an option chosen only by viewers in remote areas, with no access to traditional broadcast or cable signals. The only way these remote viewers could receive television programming was to pick it off from the networks' private satellites—the same satellites that transferred programming from network headquarters to local affiliates.

The dishes used to receive this early satellite programming were huge things, 6 or 8 feet in diameter. These dishes received signals in the C-band frequency range, between 3.4GHz and 7GHz.

Unfortunately, the attractiveness of satellite programming didn't outweigh the bulkiness of the large dishes. In addition, the networks started to encode their satellite signals, so less and less programming was legally available for free—although subscriptions were often available.

The next stage in satellite television came with the advent of smaller direct broadcast satellite (DBS) systems. These systems use more powerful geosynchronous satellites, which enable the use of smaller satellite dishes on the ground. DBS satellite dishes, offered by DIRECTV and the DISH Network, are about the size of a pizza box and can be mounted on the side or roof of a house.

Unlike the older C-band satellite signals, DBS signals are digital and are transmitted in the Ku-band range (from 12GHz to 14GHz). The digital signals make for superior picture and sound quality (compared to broadcast television or analog cable), as well as provide hundreds of specialized channels. And the geosynchronous satellites mean that dishes have to be aimed only once; they don't have to track moving satellites (or be positioned differently for different satellites), as did the older big-dish systems.

Like cable subscribers, DBS subscribers pay for various tiers of programming. DBS subscribers also have to pay for the satellite dish itself and to have it installed. This initial investment is often subsidized by the satellite providers, who provide attractive equipment packages with prepaid subscriptions.

How Satellite Signals Are Transmitted

1 The central hub of any satellite network is the broadcast center. This is where original programming is received (typically via satellite) and where the signals are converted to digital format (typically using MPEG-2 or MPEG-4 compression) and encrypted so they can't be viewed by non-paying viewers.

Broadcast center

3 The digital signal travels approximately 22,300 miles through space.

Dish

2 The broadcast center uses large satellite dishes to beam the digital signals into space. The signals are typically located in the Ku frequency range (12GHz–14GHz).

Satellites use the Ku frequency range of 12GHz–14GHz.

The Electromagnetic Spectrum

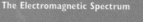

Frequency

10⁻⁶ nm	
10⁻⁵ nm	
10⁻⁴ nm	Gamma Rays
10⁻³ nm	
10⁻² nm	
10⁻¹ nm	
1 nm	X rays
10 nm	
100 nm	
10³ nm = µm	Visible Light
10 µm	
100 µm	Infrared
1000 µm = 1 mm	
10 mm = 1cm	Microwaves
10 cm	
100 cm = 1 m	Television
10 m	
100 m	
1000 m = 1 km	Radio Waves
10 km	

10 GHz

100 MHz

1 MHz

4 The digital signal bounces off one of several satellites, which are positioned in geosynchronous orbit above the Earth.

Satellite in geosynchronous orbit

5 The signals travel from the geosynchronous satellite back to Earth—another 22,300-mile trip.

6 The signals are received by a small (18"–24") round or oval satellite dish mounted to the subscriber's house, where they are then sent to the satellite receiver connected to the subscriber's television set, decrypted, and displayed onscreen.

Set-top box

TV

How Satellite Dishes Work

1 A satellite dish is nothing more than a special kind of antenna designed to receive signals beamed from satellites orbiting in space. The stand dish has a parabolic (bowl-shaped) surface and is round or oval in nature. Signals from the satellite are gathered by the dish and focused on the attached feed horn— much the same way that a concave mirror focuses light onto a central point.

Satellite dish

Feed horn

2 The feed horn receives the satellite signal. Multiple feed horns might be necessary to receive signals from separate-but-adjacent satellites or to feed multiple satellite receivers. Because signals from different satellites strike the dish at different angles, the different beams hit different feed horns.

LNB

**Adjustable
roof-mounting hardware**

Coaxial cable

Feed horns

5 The vertical position of the satellite is called the *elevation*. The elevation of a particular dish depends on how close you are to the satellite; dishes in the southern part of the United States will have a relatively high elevation (the satellite is more overhead), while those in northern states will have a lower elevation (the satellite is closer to the horizon).

4 Most consumer direct broadcast satellites are located in geosynchronous orbit over the equator, slightly west of the meridian. (For example, the main DIRECTV satellite is located at 101° west.) For this reason, the satellite dish should be pointed toward the southwest and have a clear view of the southwest sky. The horizontal position of the dish is called the *azimuth*.

3 The feed horn contains a low noise blockdown converter (LNB). The LNB amplifies the satellite signal and filters out any accompanying noise in the signal. The amplified signal from the LNB is then passed through a coaxial cable to the satellite receiver located inside the subscriber's house.

LNB (low noise blockdown) amplifies the signal and filters out radio frequency noise.

How Satellite Receivers Work

1 The final component in the satellite television system is the satellite receiver. This is a set-top box positioned near the subscriber's television set. It accepts the amplified signal from the satellite dish's LNB, via a coaxial cable input.

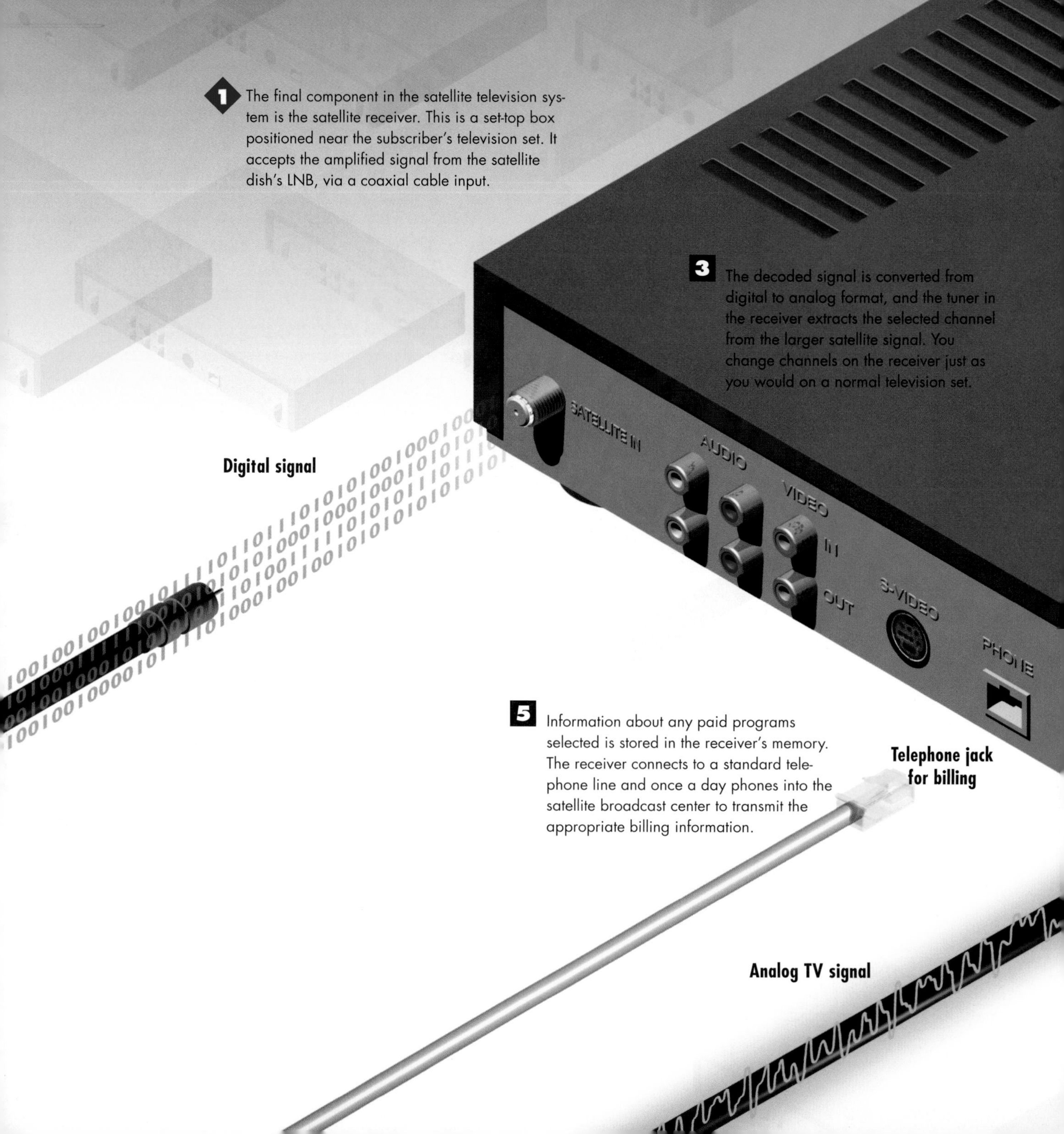

3 The decoded signal is converted from digital to analog format, and the tuner in the receiver extracts the selected channel from the larger satellite signal. You change channels on the receiver just as you would on a normal television set.

Digital signal

SATELLITE IN   AUDIO   VIDEO   IN   OUT   S-VIDEO   PHONE

5 Information about any paid programs selected is stored in the receiver's memory. The receiver connects to a standard telephone line and once a day phones into the satellite broadcast center to transmit the appropriate billing information.

Telephone jack for billing

Analog TV signal

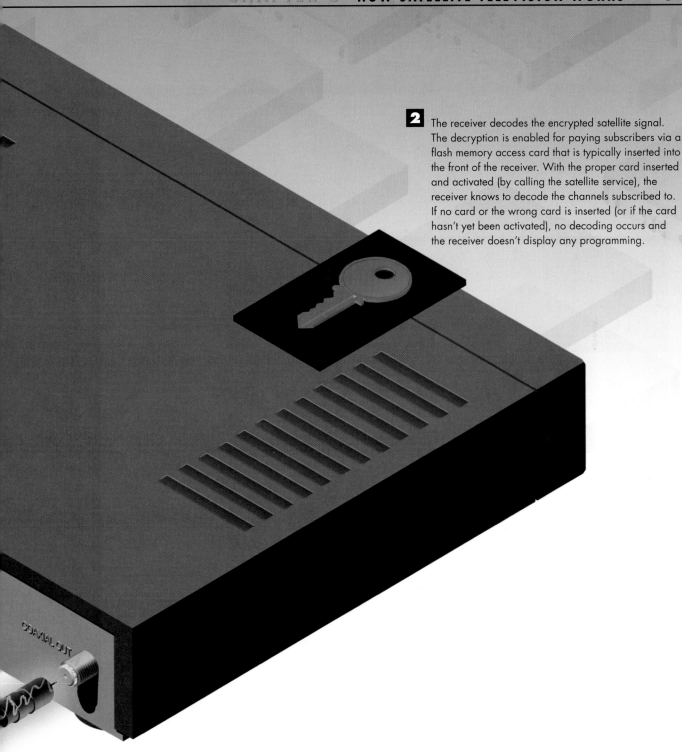

2 The receiver decodes the encrypted satellite signal. The decryption is enabled for paying subscribers via a flash memory access card that is typically inserted into the front of the receiver. With the proper card inserted and activated (by calling the satellite service), the receiver knows to decode the channels subscribed to. If no card or the wrong card is inserted (or if the card hasn't yet been activated), no decoding occurs and the receiver doesn't display any programming.

COAXIAL OUT

4 The signal for the selected channel is sent from the receiver to your television set, either via coaxial or audio/video connections.

P A R T

HOW HIGH-DEFINITION TELEVISION WORKS

OUR current NTSC television system is more than a half-century old. What was state-of-the-art in the 1950s is woefully inadequate today; today's larger television screens and higher-resolution source material require a better way to reproduce picture and sound than what we've grown used to over the years.

The first step to improving the quality of our television broadcasts is to move from analog to digital transmission. Just as digital compact discs replaced analog records, digital television will replace our outdated analog broadcasting system. Digital signals don't deteriorate as analog signals do; a digital broadcast looks every bit as good in your home as it does in the broadcast studio.

Simply digitizing a picture, however, does not improve upon a mediocre source format. To dramatically improve the picture, the format itself has to be improved. This leads us to the next step in the evolutionary process—high-definition television (HDTV). HDTV uses digital technology to increase the picture's resolution, resulting in a noticeably sharper and more life-like picture. Digital technology is also used to improve the sound quality, in the form of Dolby Digital surround sound.

In addition, the HDTV format changes the aspect ratio of the picture to more closely resemble the wide screens used in your local cinema and to better match the human field of vision, which is twice as wide as it is high. The traditional television screen has a 4:3 aspect ratio—that is, if the picture is 4 units wide, it's also 3 units tall. The HDTV format embraces a widescreen approach with a 16:9 aspect ratio—for every 16 units of width, you have just 9 units of height. The resulting picture is wider than a standard television picture and a better fit for displaying widescreen movies and other programming.

But it's not enough to say that a picture is high definition; there are actually several different HDTV formats available. For example, for broadcast television, you can find programming offered at both 720p and 1080i resolution, and some videogames offer 1080p resolution. The future high-definition DVD formats will also offer 1080p resolution. What's the difference?

It's all a matter of resolution, meaning how many lines are in the picture. The 720p format offers 720 lines of resolution, scanned progressively. The 1080i format offers 1080 lines of resolution, interlaced, and the 1080p format offers 1080 lines of resolution, scanned progressively. Any of these formats is a big improvement over the 480 lines (interlaced) offered by standard definition television.

If 1080p—the best possible HDTV picture—is possible, why bother with the other formats at all? Well, if bandwidth was unlimited and free, 1080p would always be the preferred choice. But bandwidth costs money and is often limited. That's why television broadcasters favor the 720p and 1080i formats, which use much less bandwidth than the 1080p format. In fact, 1080i is the defacto standard for HDTV broadcasts today, with only a few broadcasters (such as ESPN) favoring 720p. (That's because programming with lots of motion, such as sporting events, benefits from progressive scanning, even if the overall resolution is a tad less.)

To view 1080p programming, you'll have to wait until one of the new high-definition DVD formats arrives. Both Blu-ray Disc and HD DVD have more than enough capacity to store 1080p programming, although it's likely only one of these competing formats will survive the upcoming format wars. (And let's not forget Sony's PlayStation 3 videogame system; it's the first game console to offer 1080p output for some really great-looking games.)

One big question about HDTV is when *you'll* be able to receive HDTV signals. The reality is that viewers in most major cities can now receive digital broadcast signals from local stations representing the ABC, CBS, NBC, and FOX television networks. Several cable and satellite channels also offer HDTV programming, and the offerings are steadily growing in number.

The Federal Communications Commission (FCC) mandated that all commercial TV stations begin some form of HDTV broadcasting by May 1, 2002, offering at least half of their programs in high definition within 12 months of that date. In fact, the government wants broadcast stations to completely shift to HDTV format by 2006. While that date probably won't be met (the changeover has taken longer than originally expected), sometime soon digital broadcasts will replace analog broadcasts, and the analog broadcast spectrum will be returned to the government for some future use.

This is why most large-screen televisions sold today are capable of receiving HDTV broadcasts, either via a built-in or add-on HDTV tuner. When you buy an HDTV-capable set today, you're ready for all the HDTV programming that will be offered in the coming years. And don't worry—that new HDTV set is still compatible with all of today's analog television programming. You can watch all the traditional television programming you want and then switch to HDTV mode for the new high-resolution broadcasts.

Better picture, bigger picture, and better sound—that's what digital television and HDTV is all about. What's not to like?

CHAPTER

4

How Digital Television Works

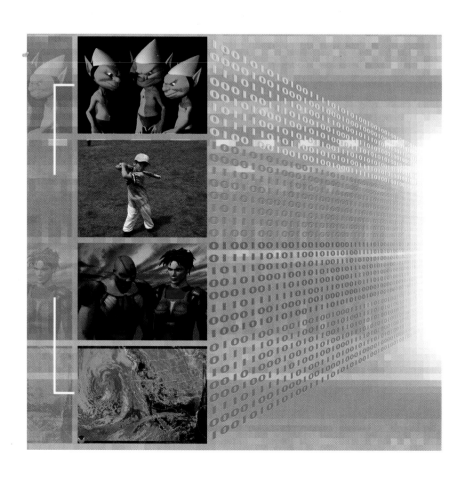

ANALOG television broadcasts transmit programming in a continuous signal that varies in amplitude, depending on the information contained in the picture. This signal can easily deteriorate or suffer interference from other sources, which produces a lower-quality picture than the original.

A digital broadcast, in contrast, converts the programming into a stream of binary on/off bits—sequences of 0s and 1s. Each bit represents a small part of the picture, and all the bits combine to reproduce a picture identical to the original.

The primary advantage of digital broadcasting is that these binary bits recombine to reproduce an exact copy of the original broadcast. Over-the-air (OTA) digital signals don't weaken, as analog signals do. As long as the signal can be received, the picture is perfect, with no degradation or ghosting. Because digital signals are comprised of binary bits, a 1 is always a 1 and a 0 is always a 0. Because of this exact end-to-end reproduction, digital means better picture and sound quality, no matter what is broadcast.

It's important to note again that digital television is not the same as high-definition television. While all HDTV is digital, not all digital broadcasts are high-definition. (It's kind of like the old pasta analogy—while all spaghetti is pasta, not all pasta is spaghetti.) Digital technology is used in a variety of media, including DVDs, direct broadcast satellite (DBS), digital cable, and the new HDTV format.

For broadcasting purposes, the FCC has allocated 19.39 megabits per second (Mbps) of bandwidth for each digital channel. This bandwidth can be used in a number of ways—for a single high-definition channel or for multiple subchannels. When used for multicasting, each subchannel can carry a complete standard definition program (in digital format) or specific data streams. This means that broadcasters can offer a variety of special data services over their digital channels, in addition to their normal programming. For example, a station might offer HDTV programming on one subchannel, an SD version of that programming on a second subchannel, a local news or weather feed (in standard definition) on a third subchannel, and a continuous weather radar feed on a fourth subchannel.

How Digital Signals Work

1 With analog signals, the height (amplitude) of the radio wave represents various aspects of the broadcast, such as color, brightness, and so on. Digital signals carry this same information, but encoded as a series of binary digital bits—groupings of 0s and 1s.

HDTV

MPEG compression

Multiple SDTV video streams

4 The 19.39Mbps digital stream can also be divided into several streams, called *subchannels*, each with its own programming. For example, one 19.39Mbps channel can carry four 4.85Mbps subchannels. Subchannels can be used for standard definition programming or for other types of digital data, such as news tickers or audio channels. If the digital television channel is channel 51, the subchannels would be designated 51.1, 51.2, 51.3, and so on.

MPEG compression

2 The digital signal is broadcast over a channel that can transmit 19.39Mbps. This digital stream can carry a variety of types of digital information.

HDTV

19.39Mbps

3 For high-definition television broadcasts, the entire 19.39Mbps digital stream can be dedicated to a single program.

19.39Mbps total

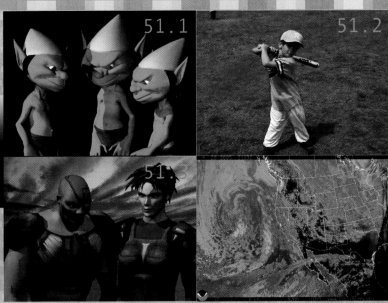

51.1   51.2

51.3

5 The digital signal is received by the tuner/decoder in your digital television set. The decoder portion of the tuner—essentially a small computer—reassembles the digital bits into video and audio signals that are then displayed by your television.

Multiple SDTV video streams

How Different Digital Formats Compare

1 **SDTV**—Standard definition digital television has the same resolution and aspect ratio as analog television but is transmitted in digital fashion. The SDTV picture is 480 × 640 pixels, with interlaced scanning.

SDTV

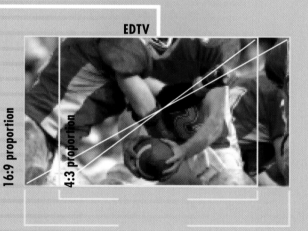

4:3 proportion

2 **EDTV**—Enhanced definition television has the same resolution as SDTV but with progressive scanning for a smoother overall picture. EDTV can be in either the 4:3 or 16:9 aspect ratio, for a resolution of either 480 × 640 or 480 × 720 pixels.

EDTV

16:9 proportion

4:3 proportion

Name	NTSC	SDTV	EDTV	EDTV	HDTV	HDTV	HDTV
Description	480i (analog)	480i (digital)	480p	480p (widescreen)	720p	1080i	1080p
Transmission type	Analog	Digital	Digital	Digital	Digital	Digital	Digital
Aspect ratio	4:3	4:3	4:3	16:9	16:9	16:9	16:9
Picture height (pixels)	480	480	480	480	720	1080	1080
Picture width (pixels)	640	640	640	720	1280	1920	1920
Total number of pixels	307,200	307,200	307,200	345,600	921,600	2,073,600	2,073,600
Scanning	Interlaced	Interlaced	Progressive	Progressive	Progressive	Interlaced	Progressive
Used by	Standard television	DVD, direct broadcast satellite, digital cable	Progressive-scan DVD	Progressive-scan DVD	HD broadcasts (ABC, ESPN, Fox)	HD broadcasts (CBS, DiscoveryHD, HBO, HDNet, NBC, PBS, Showtime, UPN, WB)	PS3 video games, future high-definition DVD formats

3 **HDTV (720p)**—The first of the two current high-definition television formats features 720 × 1280 pixel resolution with progressive scanning. This format is ideal for programming with lots of movement, such as sporting events.

HDTV 720p

16:9 proportion

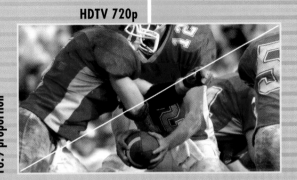

4 **HDTV (1080i)**—The second current high-definition format features greater resolution (1080 × 1920 pixels) but with interlaced scanning. Both the 720p and 1080i formats feature a 16:9 aspect ratio and Dolby Digital 5.1 surround sound.

HDTV 1080i

16:9 proportion

5 **HDTV (1080p)**—This is the ultimate high-definition format, with 1080 × 1920 pixel resolution and progressive scanning. Because of the high bandwidth requirements, this format is not yet in use for high-definition television broadcasts. It is, however, an option when playing PS3 games and it likely to be used in next-generation high-definition DVDs.

HDTV 1080p

16:9 proportion

How Progressive Scanning Works

1 Normal television pictures are composed of 480 horizontal lines that scan across the screen in less than the blink of an eye. The conventional way of putting the lines onscreen is to display two sequential fields of 240 lines each; each odd and even field is scanned in 1/60th of a second. This *interlaced scanning* process is used for all analog broadcasts, as well as the 1080i HDTV format. The 1080i format utilizes two sequential fields of 540 lines each.

Interlaced scanning Lines

30 frames (60 fields) per second

2 Interlaced scanning produces 60 fields or 30 complete frames every second. This slower refresh rate results in some flickering of the picture, especially with larger screen sizes.

3 A more visually appealing approach is to scan all the horizontal lines in a single pass. This *progressive scanning* process flashes the complete picture onscreen in 1/60th of a second, as opposed to the half-picture fields displayed with interlaced scanning. The result is improved picture quality; even though the resolution (number of pixels) remains the same, the picture is refreshed twice as quickly. Progressive scanning is used for the 480p EDTV format, the 720p HDTV format, and for the future 1080p HDTV format.

Progressive Scan DVD Players
Progressive scanning is most often encountered when examining DVD players. Most newer DVD players are capable of interpolating the missing lines in each half-picture field, using a technology called *line doubling*, which turns an interlaced 480-line picture into a noticeably sharper progressive-scanned 480-line picture. The newly created 480p picture must be fed from the DVD player via a component video, DVI, or HDMI connection; the standard composite video or S-Video connection can only transmit the original 480i picture.

Lines **Progressive scanning**

60 full frames per second

4 Progressive scanning produces 60 complete frames every second—twice as many as an interlaced picture. This translates into a more accurate display when you have fast action onscreen, such as with sporting events.

How Digital Compression Works

1 Digital compression works by separating successive frames into two types of video information—that which stays the same from frame to frame and that which changes from frame to frame. Because the static information doesn't have to be redrawn from scratch in each successive frame, the video signal is compressed to use less bandwidth. The whole process starts with the first frame in a sequence, called an *intraframe (I-frame)*, which is a single compressed frame that contains all the spatial information of a video frame. An I-frame is encoded as a single freestanding image, with no reference to preceding or subsequent frames.

2 *Predictive frames (P-frames)* are computed frames, based on the nearest previous I- or P-frame. The P-frame is calculated by comparing the previous and successive frames and recording only the changes in the picture. P-frames are more highly compressed than I-frames and provide a reference for the calculation of B-frames.

...ne
(...nly)

I - frame
(Keyframe)

P - frame
(Changes Only)

B - frame   **B - frame**   **B - frame**   **B - frame**   **B - frame**

3 *Bi-directional frames (B-frames)* use both past and subsequent frames as references to calculate the compressed frame data.

4 The final video picture is composed of the first I-frame and the changed information represented by each successive P-frame.

Displayed image

P - frame
(Changes Only)

P - frame
(Changes Only)

I -
(Key

B - frame

B - frame

B - frame

B - fr

MPEG Compression

To fit all the information of an EDTV or HDTV signal into as little bandwidth as possible, the digital signal must be compressed. The most common compression technologies are the MPEG-2 and MPEG-4 processes, which work by identifying and removing redundant information between successive frames of the picture. Only the picture information that has changed is recorded; static information is stored in memory and repeated until it changes. By recording only the changed information, the compression ratio approaches 40:1.

Up to 40:1 video stream compression

CHAPTER

5

How HDTV Works

HIGH-DEFINITION television (HDTV) is just one form of digital broadcasting—but it's the best one. The HDTV format combines several technologies to offer a bigger, higher-resolution picture and sound field.

There are several reasons HDTV is appealing to both videophiles and normal consumers. All the reasons tend to boil down to a better viewing experience, and include

■ **Sharper picture**—True HDTV (720p or 1080i formats) delivers one million pixels or more of information. Standard TV and DVDs deliver approximately 300,000 pixels. That translates into HDTV delivering a picture more than three times as detailed as what you're used to watching.

■ **Less flicker**—The increased number of scan lines per frame (and, in the case of the 720p format, progressive scanning) translates into less-visible scan lines—which means you can sit closer to the screen without seeing flicker in the picture.

■ **More accurate widescreen reproduction**—When you display a widescreen movie on a standard 4:3 television, the movie is either letterboxed (with black bars at the top and bottom of the screen) or panned and scanned so that only a portion of the movie is displayed onscreen. With HDTV's 16:9 aspect ration, you can see more of the widescreen movie with less letterboxing.

■ **Increased picture fidelity**—Because HDTV uses digital transmission, the original picture is faithfully reproduced on the receiving end—there's no deterioration of the picture over long distances or with time. What you see is what was originally recorded or broadcast.

■ **Better sound**—The HDTV format dictates the Dolby Digital 5.1 surround sound format, which is much improved over the NTSC stereo standard. Dolby Digital and all that is audio is covered in Part IV, "How Audio Works."

How the Components of HDTV Work Together

1 **Digital transmission**—All HDTV signals are encoded and transmitted digitally, via a series of binary bits. This results in exact fidelity to the original programming source.

3 **Digital video compression**—To fit the increased pixels of the HDTV picture into the allotted bandwidth, MPEG-2 or MPEG-4 digital compression is used to fit more bits into the same amount of space. Only changed parts of the picture are encoded; redundant bits of the picture are not transmitted.

4:3

16:9 aspect ratio

4 **Widescreen display**—SDTV utilizes a squarish 4:3 ratio screen, which is ill-suited for viewing widescreen movies of HD content. HDTV uses a 16:9 ratio widescreen display—perfect for movies and other widescreen programming.

2 **Higher resolution**—A standard definition television (SDTV) picture is composed of approximately 300,000 pixels. The HDTV picture is composed of either 921,000 or slightly more than 2 million pixels (depending on the format)—for more than three times the picture information. This results in a much more detailed picture.

5 **Digital surround sound**— The standard NTSC system allows for analog stereo sound, with rudimentary Dolby Pro Logic matrixed surround sound. The HDTV system incorporates the state-of-the-art Dolby Digital surround sound system, with pristine digital sound reproduced in a 5.1-channel system.

How HDTV Reproduces a Better Picture

1 Images viewed on television screens are made up of small picture elements known as *pixels*. Each pixel is comprised of three closely spaced dots of color—red, green, and blue. The easiest way to increase picture resolution is to stuff more of these pixels onto the screen, by using smaller pixels. In the 1080i format, 18 HDTV pixels can fit in the same space occupied by 4 pixels used in traditional television sets.

In the same space as

4 SDTV pixels

18 HDTV pixels

SDTV

307,200 pixels

Pixel Measurements

A *pixel* (short for "picture element") is a single point onscreen. Video displays are created from thousands (or millions) of pixels, arranged in rows and columns. The pixels are so close together that, from the proper distance, they appear connected and create a complete picture.

2 HDTV pixels are not just smaller than SDTV pixels; they're also squarer. This enables an HDTV display to resolve finer details and hold smoother curves. The square pixels also remove some of the image distortion seen on older televisions.

HDTV pixel

SDTV scan line pixel

HDTV

3 By using these smaller, squarer pixels, an HDTV picture can contain up to seven times the total number of pixels found in a standard definition picture. The 1080i format uses more than 2 million individual pixels—compared with just 300,000 pixels in a traditional television screen.

2,073,600 pixels

How HDTV Signals Are Transmitted

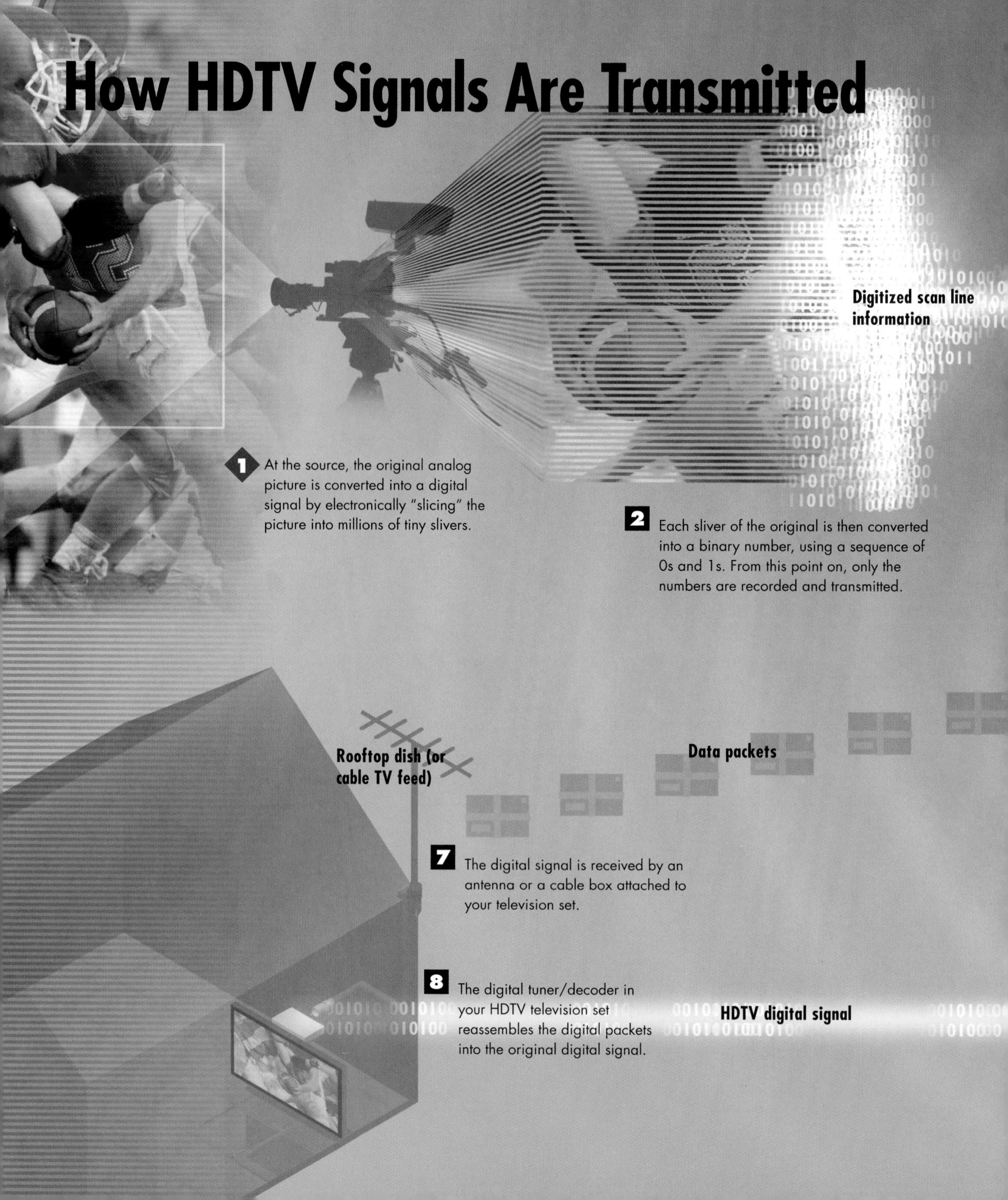

Digitized scan line information

1 At the source, the original analog picture is converted into a digital signal by electronically "slicing" the picture into millions of tiny slivers.

2 Each sliver of the original is then converted into a binary number, using a sequence of 0s and 1s. From this point on, only the numbers are recorded and transmitted.

Rooftop dish (or cable TV feed)

Data packets

7 The digital signal is received by an antenna or a cable box attached to your television set.

8 The digital tuner/decoder in your HDTV television set reassembles the digital packets into the original digital signal.

HDTV digital signal

Geosynchronous satellite

3 The digital data stream is now compressed to a 45Mbps stream for broadcasting to affiliate stations over a Ku-band satellite.

4 The local station receives the digital data stream via a large satellite dish.

6 The digital data is broken into a series of packets (incorporating error correction) for over-the-air or cable transmission.

5 The digital data stream is now processed through an MPEG-2 or MPEG-4 digital encoder with a data output rate of 19.39Mbps.

9 The digital signal is now decoded to reproduce the original source programming and is fed to your HDTV television display.

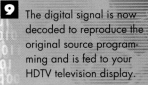

HDTV

CHAPTER

6

How Screen Aspect Ratios Work

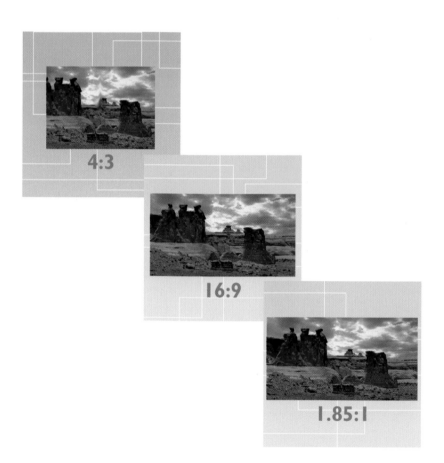

4:3

16:9

1.85:1

ORIGINALLY, all motion pictures were projected on a squarish screen with an aspect ratio of 4:3—which means that if a screen is four units of measurement wide, it's also three units tall. (Another way to express this aspect ratio is 1.33:1, meaning the width is 1.33 times the height.) When television was first developed, it adopted this same 4:3 aspect ratio.

When the movie industry began to feel threatened by the rise of television in the 1950s, Hollywood responded by producing films in various widescreen formats, which better represented the wide human field of vision. These formats—Panavision, Cinemascope, and the rest—provided a much wider picture than that presented by television's "little square box," with aspect ratios ranging from 1.66:1 to 2.76:1. In the widest of these formats, the picture is almost three times as wide as it was tall. How, then, does one display widescreen movies on a non-widescreen television?

There are two ways this can work. The most common, until recently, is for a technician to "pan and scan" the narrower television image area over the movie's image, cutting off the edges of the widescreen picture. The result isn't always satisfactory, however, because it often cuts off important parts of the picture and definitely interferes with the way the director wanted the movie presented.

A more recent approach is to present the movie at its full width, which leaves some unused areas at the top and bottom of your television screen. This approach, called *letterboxing*, displays the widescreen movie in a strip across the center of your screen, with long black bars above and below the movie image.

A better solution is to use a widescreen television display, like the 16:9 (1.78:1) aspect ratio screens used in today's latest HDTV sets. With this aspect ratio, widescreen movies that use the common 1.85:1 ratio can be displayed on a screen with little or no letterboxing; even the wider 2.35:1 movies fit better on a screen with a 1.78:1 ratio!

How Different Aspect Ratios Compare

1 **4:3 ratio**—This ratio is also referred to as 1.33:1 or the *Academy ratio*. This format was the shape of virtually all movies prior to the 1950s and is the shape of traditional television programming. This is also the aspect ratio used by all non-HD television sets.

4:3

2 **1.66:1**—This aspect ratio isn't widely used by American moviemakers, with the notable exception of cartoons and animated features, such as Disney's *The Little Mermaid*. Many European movies, however, are made in this aspect ratio.

1.66:1

3 **16:9**—Also referred to as 1.78:1, this is the aspect ratio adopted by the HDTV format, and it is used in all high-definition television displays.

16:9

4 **1.85:1**—Sometimes referred to as *Academy flat*, this is the aspect ratio used by most American movies today.

1.85:1

Cinematic Widescreen Processes

Over the years, Hollywood has used a variety of widescreen processes, each with a slightly different aspect ratio. These processes have included Cinerama (2.60:1), CinemaScope (2.35:1, 2.55:1, and 2.66:1), Panavision (2.40:1), Super Panavision 70 (2.20:1), Technirama (2.20:1 and 2.35:1), Todd-AO (2.35:1), Ultra Panavision 70 (2.35:1 and 2.76:1), and VistaVision (1.66:1, 1.85:1, and 2.0:1).

Cinerama
(2:60:1)

CinemaScope
(2.35:1, 2.55:1, 2:66:1)

Panavision
(2.40:1)

5 **2.35:1**—This aspect ratio is used by many epic movies and musicals. This is the aspect ratio used in the CinemaScope, Technirama, Todd-AO, and Ultra Panavision 70 movie systems. All the *Star Wars* movies were shot in this aspect ratio.

6 **2.60:1**—This ultra-widescreen format was used by the Cinerama system, as typified by the epic movie *How the West Was Won*.

2.35:1

2.60:1

8 **Open matte**—The open matte process involves shooting a large frame, which is then matted from the sides for 4:3 prints and from the top and bottom for 1.85:1 prints. The visible part of the picture is thus slightly different depending on the final aspect ratio.

7 **2.76:1**—Another ultra-widescreen format, this was used for 70mm Ultra Panavision 70 prints. This aspect ratio was used for films such as *Ben Hur* and *It's a Mad, Mad, Mad, Mad World*.

2.76:1

4:3

1.85:1

Oversize frame for cropping

| Super Panavision (2.20:1) | Technirama (2.20:1, 2.35:1) | Todd-AO (2.35:1) | Ultra Panavision 70 (2.35:1, 2.76:1) | VistaVision (1.66:1, 1.85:1, 2.0:1) |

How Letterboxing Works

1 **Pan and scan**—Before letterboxing, widescreen movies were subjected to the pan and scan technique, in which the sides of the image area are cropped off to fit the 4:3 Academy ratio. This technique cuts up to 45% of the total picture area, often resulting in major characters being trimmed from the frame.

2.35:1
movie
frame

Pan and scan moves the 4:3 window within a larger frame to capture the area of interest.

2 **Letterboxing for 4:3 displays—**
Letterboxing displays the widescreen picture at
its full width, with black bars filling the screen
above and below the picture. This results in the
movie being displayed as the director intended,
although some viewers complain about the
smaller overall picture (especially on smaller-
sized screens) and the "wasted" area of the
black bars.

3 **Letterboxing for 16:9
displays—**HDTV's 16:9
(1.78:1) aspect ratio minimizes
the letterbox effect, although
some letterboxing is still required
for movies shot at the 1.85:1 or
2.35:1 ratio.

How 4:3 Programming Is Displayed on a 16:9 Screen

1 **Windowpane mode**—To preserve the original aspect ratio, 4:3 programming can be displayed on a 16:9 screen with black or gray bars on either side of the picture. This technique is known as *windowpaning* or *pillarboxing*; it's effectively the opposite of letterboxing for widescreen movies.

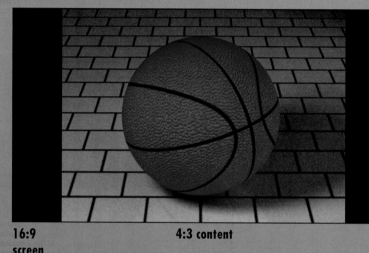

16:9
screen   4:3 content

2 **Stretch mode**—Many viewers prefer to stretch the 4:3 programming to fill the entire width of the widescreen display. This results in a somewhat distorted picture, however—people and objects tend to look short and fat.

Letterbox and Windowpane Burn-in
Some types of video displays—notably CRT and plasma flat panels—can suffer burn-in if the blank stripes of a windowpaned or letterboxed picture are left on the screen for extended periods of time. If you have a CRT or plasma display, you should avoid windowpane and letterbox modes, instead opting for one of the stretch modes. Other display types—including DLP projectors and DLP flat panels—do not suffer burn-in and are recommended if you prefer to watch 4:3 material in the windowpane mode.

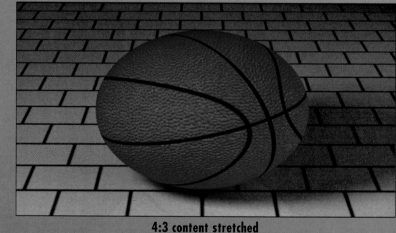

4:3 content stretched

3 **Smart stretch mode**—Some televisions feature a "smart" expand mode. This process maintains the original aspect ratio for the center portion of the picture, stretching only the edges of the picture to fill the entire widescreen display. The result appears somewhat less distorted than normal stretching.

Stretched area

Stretched area

Cropped area

4 **Zoom mode**—Another option is the zoom mode, which enlarges the entire 4:3 picture to fill the entire width of the widescreen display. This process results in some cropping of the top and bottom of the original picture, though.

Cropped area

How Anamorphic Widescreen DVDs Work

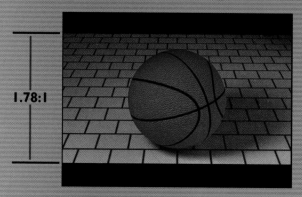

1.78:1

1 When a widescreen movie is letterboxed to fit a 4:3 display, black bars are added above and below the picture. By default, these black bars utilize the necessary scan lines in the picture frame, thus "wasting" those lines for this non-important picture information.

2 When the letterboxed 4:3 picture is shown on a 16:9 display, you end up with a combination of letterboxing and windowpaning—that is, black stripes above and below the picture, as well as black or gray stripes on either side. The picture itself fills up only a portion of the total screen.

3 If you use your television's zoom mode to enlarge the picture, it appears to be of lower resolution—which it is. That's because you've lost those scan lines devoted to the letterboxed area of the screen. For example, a picture with a 2.35:1 aspect ratio only uses 272 of the 480 possible scan lines (on a DVD) for the movie itself; the remaining 218 scan lines are wasted on the black letterbox bars. So, when you enlarge the picture to fill a 16:9 screen, you're watching a picture with just 272 lines of resolution!

Just 272 out of 480 scan lines used to display image

4 The solution to this problem is to use a technique called *anamorphic widescreen*, which is part of the DVD standard. On an anamorphic DVD, a widescreen picture is not letterboxed on the disc, so no scan lines are wasted on the black bars.

5 Instead, an anamorphic lens is used to squeeze the full picture 33% horizontally, to fit a 4:3 frame. If you were to watch the movie without proper processing, everything would look tall and skinny.

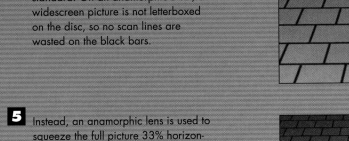

6 When your DVD player plays an anamorphic image, it automatically stretches the picture 33% to fit a 16:9 display. Because the resulting picture uses the full 480 scan lines of the DVD format (no scan lines wasted on letterboxing), it looks much sharper than a nonanamorphic picture zoomed to fit the same screen.

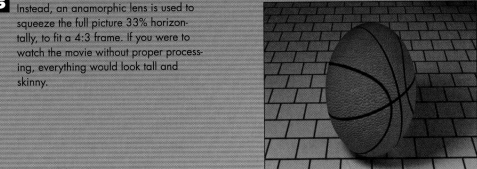

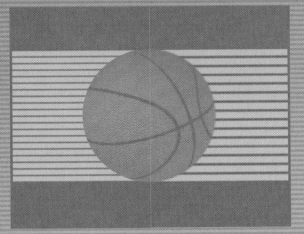

7 When you play an anamorphic DVD on a 4:3 ratio screen, your DVD player squeezes the picture 33% vertically. Black letterbox bars are automatically added at the top and the bottom to fill the blank space.

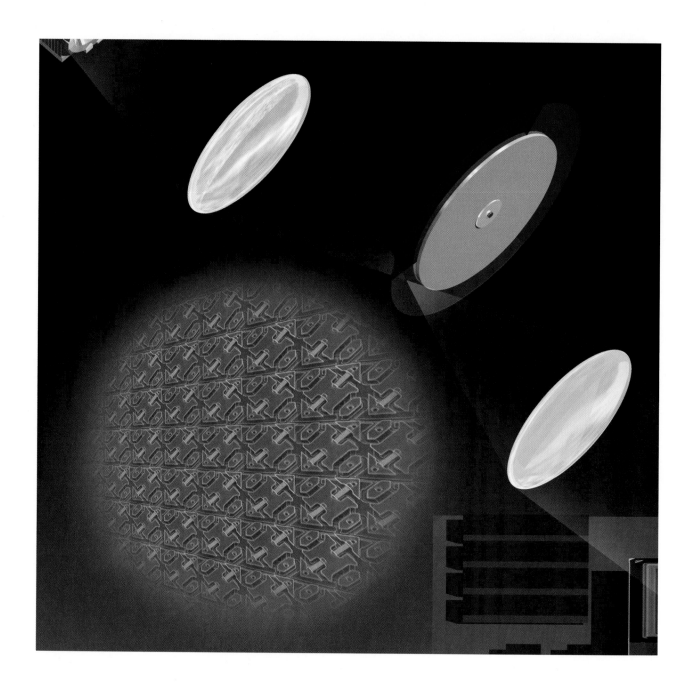

P A R T

HOW VIDEO DISPLAYS WORK

THE most important part of your home theater system is the video display. The better—and bigger—your video display, the more realistic your home theater experience.

Today's state-of-the-art video displays are much different from the simple television sets of yesteryear. Not only are they bigger and shaped differently (wide-screen versus squarish), they're also capable of reproducing the high-resolution pictures broadcast in the new HDTV format. If you're purchasing a new home theater system, plan on allocating at least a quarter of your budget to the video display.

Also unlike the past, today you can choose from four types of displays—and various technologies behind each display type. Which technology and type of display you choose depends on your budget, the demands of your room, and your personal preferences.

Direct-View

Direct-view displays are the traditional type of television sets you've always had in your living room. A direct-view television uses a picture tube—also called a cathode ray tube (CRT)—as its video display; you can find direct-view sets as small as 5" (measured diagonally) and as large as 40".

Direct-view sets typically have the brightest picture of any display type and generally cost less than similar-sized projection or flat-panel sets. Their main limitation is size; if your viewing distance is 10' or more, a direct-view set might be inadequate for your needs. In addition, direct-view sets are bigger (front to back) and heavier than other displays, so factor that into your decision.

Rear Projection

Rear projection televisions (RPTVs) are ideal for viewers who have a bigger room and need a bigger screen than what you can get in a direct-view set but don't want to totally break the bank.

Today's lowest-priced RPTV models use older CRT technology, in which the picture is produced by three small, internal picture tubes. These sets produce a high-resolution picture but lack the brightness of newer technologies. (They're also big and bulky.)

Newer RPTVs use various microdisplay technologies, such as digital light projection (DLP), liquid crystal display (LCD), and liquid crystal on silicon (LCoS) to create a picture from a much smaller internal light engine. The result is a brighter picture than a CRT-based RPTV, but in a smaller, lighter cabinet. Microdisplay RPTVs are available in sizes ranging from 42" to 7" and provide consumers with a big picture at a relatively low cost, which is why they're so popular today.

There are some downsides to microdisplay technologies, however. First, microdisplay sets typically cost a little more than similar-sized CRT-based units. Second, all microdisplay sets use a high-intensity bulb that burns out over time. (The bulb itself is typically good for thousands of hours of viewing and is user-replaceable, though.)

Third, some microdisplay technologies have technological limitations. For example, the black levels on some LCD RPTVs aren't as dark as with other microdisplays. And DLP RPTVs can produce a "rainbow" effect that is visible to some sensitive viewers. All of which means you'll need to carefully evaluate the available technologies before you make a buying decision.

Front Projection

Front projection televisions (FPTVs) are used in most larger and professional home theater installations. The advantage of an FPTV is that you can project a *really* large picture—up to 20' diagonal in some super installations.

An FPTV system works similarly to an RPTV system, except the internal light engine (CRT, LCD, or DLP) sits in front of the screen, typically behind the audience, and projects the picture across the room directly onto the screen. This type of system is inherently less bright than any other type of display (although newer generations are much better than older models) and has a somewhat narrow viewing angle. This means that the room has to be relatively dark and narrow for an FPTV system to work—although the room can be very large, of course. Price varies considerably by model and function; some bargain front projectors are lower-priced than RPTV sets, while higher-end models can run into the five figures.

Flat-panel

The newest type of display is very thin—and very expensive. These displays are thin and light enough to hang on a wall. While flat-panel displays are attractive from an interior design standpoint, they're typically more expensive than similar RPTV displays.

Two types of flat-panel displays are available today. Plasma displays are typically larger (42"–60"), while LCD displays are typically smaller (13"–50"), although they're starting to meet in the middle ground. Even though plasma is extremely popular, it's not a good choice if you're worried about screen burn-in; static images (such as network logos or letterbox bars) leave a ghost image if displayed for too long. LCD displays have no burn-in problems but aren't quite as good at displaying deep blacks. Either type of display is attractive from a design standpoint, although somewhat expensive.

Resolution

In addition to choosing a display technology, you also need to choose a display resolution. Not every high-resolution display is the same resolution—some displays are higher definition than others.

Look for the "native resolution" of a display to be expressed in pixels, typically as width times height, or sometimes vice versa. The minimum resolution you want in an HD display is 720×1280 pixels, otherwise known as 720p resolution. Some higher-end displays now offer 1080×1920 pixel resolution, which is what is required to reproduce a true 1080p picture. Obviously, the higher the resolution, the better the picture.

CHAPTER
7

How Direct-View
Televisions Work

THE most popular video display continues to be the old standby—direct-view. Direct-view televisions have been around as long as television itself, and they are in no danger of being supplanted by any of the other display formats. In fact, the most popular screen size remains the good old 20-incher—which you can now buy for $100 or less.

The standard direct-view TV includes a picture tube, also called a *cathode ray tube (CRT)*; a tuner for receiving over-the-air television signals; the various circuitry it takes to convert the television signals into the images displayed on the CRT; and a sound system consisting of one or more speakers. A direct-view television set is not much different today from the models produced 10 or 20 or even 50 years ago—they're just higher quality and lower priced.

Direct-view TVs are ideal for budget and midrange home theater systems because they deliver the brightest picture and the widest viewing angle at the lowest cost of any available display device. The only limitation to direct-view television is the screen size; today's direct-view sets top off at 40" diagonal (for a 4:3 screen; the largest 16:9 screen is 38" diagonal), while rear projection sets can go to 60" or even 70" for a 16:9 screen.

You can, however, find direct-view televisions capable of displaying high-definition programming, complete with 16:9-ratio widescreen CRTs. Many higher-end direct-view sets also have two or more speakers for stereo sound and a plethora of input and output jacks to connect other audio/video devices (such as DVD players and satellite receivers).

Today's best direct-view TVs are unmatched in picture quality by any other display technology. A state-of-the-art CRT produces a sharper, higher-resolution picture than any projection or flat panel display does. They might seem old-fashioned in today's world of high-tech displays, but direct-view CRT televisions continue to deliver!

How a Cathode-ray Tube Works

1 A cathode-ray tube is a large vacuum tube—literally, a glass tube with a vacuum inside. The tube itself has a conductive coating, which soaks up the electrons that pile up on the face of the tube.

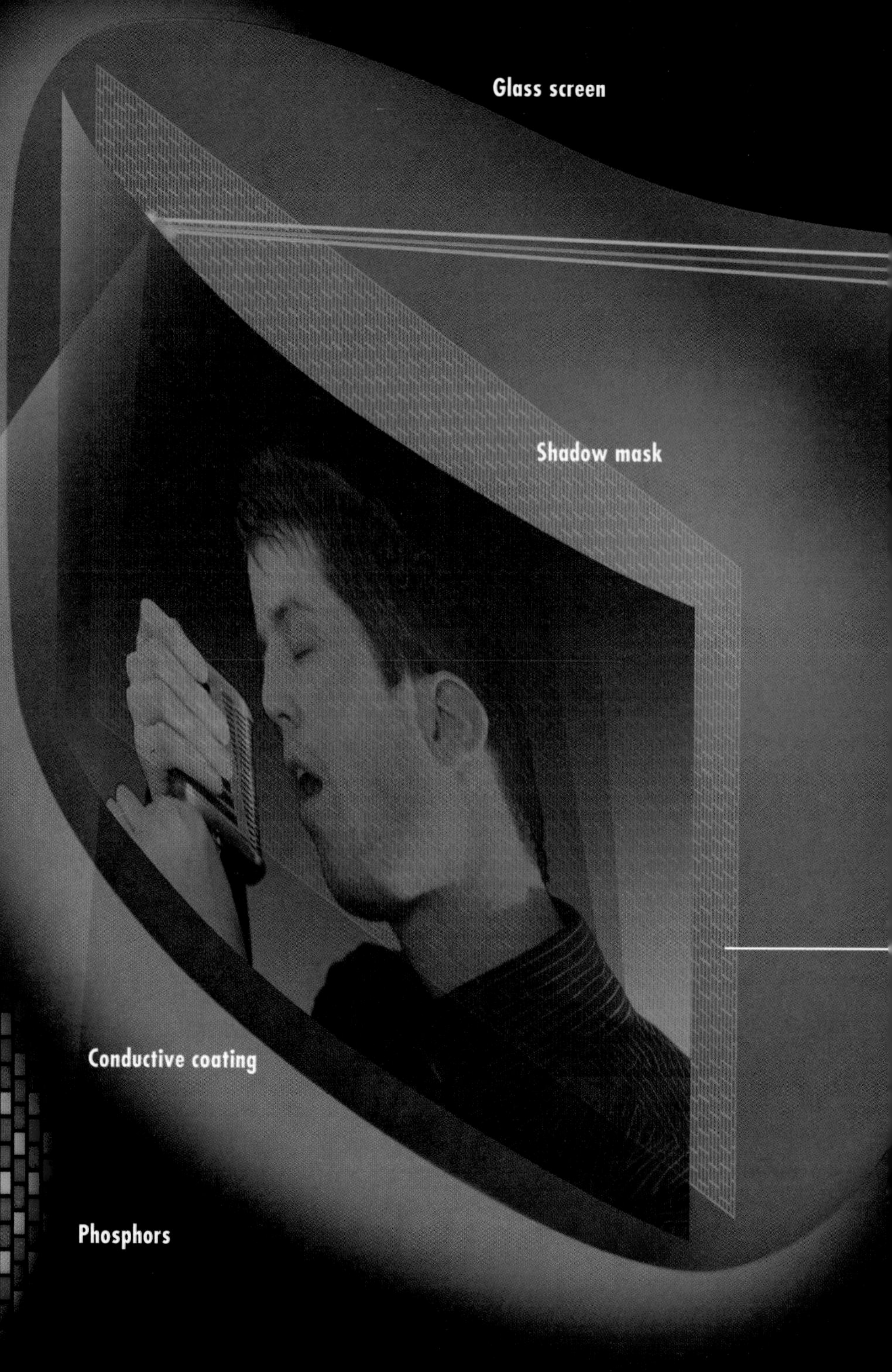

6 The glass of the CRT is coated with a layer of phosphors, which emit visible light when exposed to radiation; different types of phosphors emit different colors. When the electrons hit the phosphor coating, each phosphor dot or stripe glows in turn, producing the desired point of color.

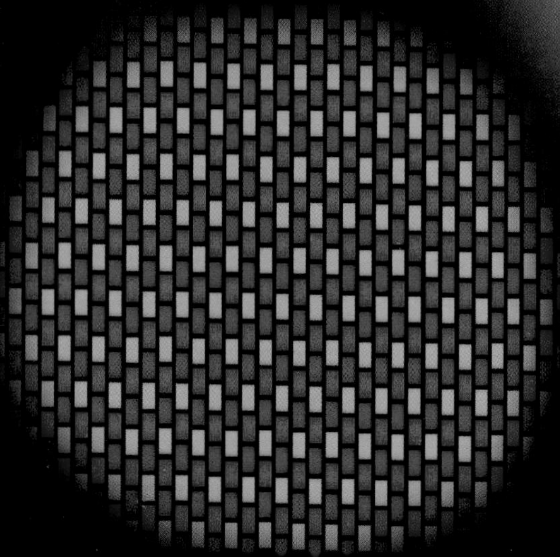

Glass screen

Shadow mask

Conductive coating

Phosphors

2 The cathode part of the cathode-ray tube is a heated filament, like the filament in a normal light bulb, that acts as a negative terminal. As the cathode is heated, electrons are produced. The number of electrons produced is controlled by the voltage level applied; the higher the voltage, the more electrons—and the brighter the resulting electron beam.

Beam deflection yoke

Electron gun

Cathode

Anode

Electron beams (red, green, and blue)

3 The negatively charged electrons are attracted to and moved forward by a positively charged anode. The anode serves as an electron gun to focus the electrons into three separate high-speed beams: red, green, and blue.

4 A set of magnetic coils called the *deflection yoke* effectively "steers" the electron beam, pointing it toward the front surface of the CRT. One set of coils creates a magnetic field that moves the beam vertically, while another set of coils moves the beam horizontally. In this fashion the steered beam paints a grid, or *raster*, pattern across the screen. For an interlaced standard definition display, the entire screen is painted 60 times per second—30 times for the odd-numbered lines and another 30 times for the even-numbered lines.

5 Each electron beam passes through tiny holes in the *shadow mask*, a metal sheet with a grid of small holes that are aligned with a similar pattern of phosphors on the face of the CRT. The shadow mask focuses each beam on the appropriate red, green, or blue phosphor dot.

How to Make a Flatter, Slimmer CRT

1 From the 1940s through the 1960s, vacuum tube manufacturing technology dictated that glass picture tubes be round in shape. The rounded corners cut off significant areas of the picture, and the curved front surface created some degree of picture distortion.

2 Continuing advances in vacuum tube manufacturing technology eventually enabled the creation of picture tubes with squared corners, so that less picture information was cut off. The front surface of the tube, however, retained its curved contours because the electron beam was a fixed length between the electron gun and the front of the tube.

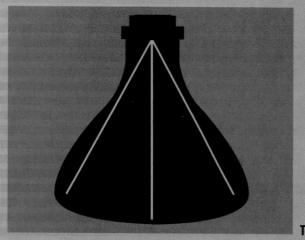

Top

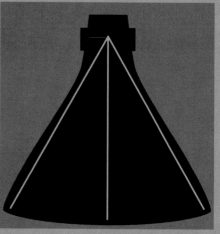

Top

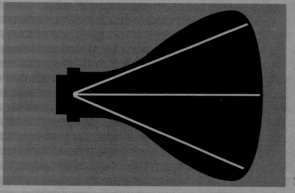

Side

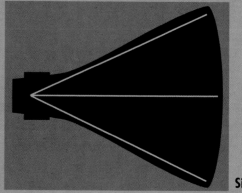

Side

Original CRT technology

Front

Modern CRT technology

Front

Smaller,
round screen

Somewhat larger,
flatter screen

Larger, flatter screen

1940   1970   2000

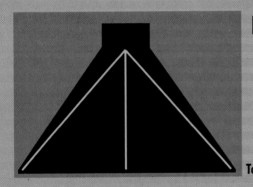

Top

3 To reduce or totally remove the CRT's curved front surface, a special electron gun is used. This electron gun is capable of creating electron beams of varying lengths. Shorter beams are shot toward the center of the screen, while longer beams are shot toward the edges. This enables the use of picture tubes with totally flat front surfaces, without the picture warping or distorting.

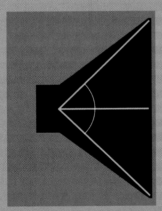

Side

4 Traditionally, the electron gun on the neck of the picture tube was positioned at a 90° angle to the front surface of the CRT—the larger the screen size, the deeper the tube. To produce a slimmer tube, a special electronic gun is used that operates at a 110° angle, thus shortening the neck of the CRT by several inches.

New flatter, slimmer technology

Front

CHAPTER

8

How Rear Projection Televisions Work

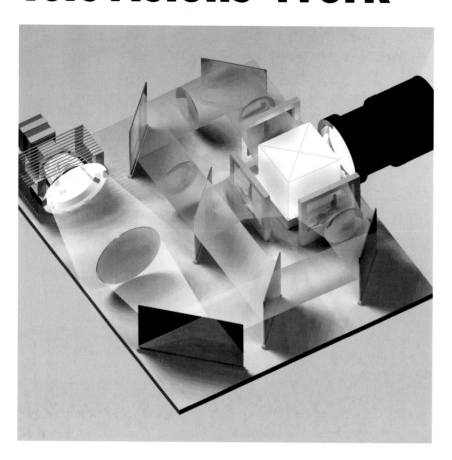

WHEN you want a larger display for a bigger room (anything over 40'' diagonal), you need to step up from a direct view to a rear projection display. For most home theater enthusiasts, a rear projection television (RPTV) is the best choice for their main video display. RPTVs present a good value in terms of price and performance and come in the right sizes for most living rooms.

Today's RPTVs are much better than models sold even a few years ago. If you're used to the fuzzy picture on the projection TV in your local bar, you're in for a big surprise. The best RPTVs today deliver pictures that rival those from similar-sized direct view TVs.

That's because today's RPTVs use more advanced technology than the RPTVs of the past. While some low-priced models are still based on internal CRT technology, newer models use microdisplay technology that produces a brighter picture from a smaller internal light engine; these DLP and LCD projection sets are much smaller and lighter than comparable CRT-based RPTVs.

The main advantages of RPTVs are a larger picture size (compared to direct view), relatively low cost, and increased room flexibility (when compared to front projection TVs). The main disadvantage to RPTVs is size, especially with CRT-based models. Also, screen brightness, even with the best models, isn't quite as good as with direct-view sets; some RPTVs can look a little washed out under direct lighting and have a slightly more limited viewing angle.

Most RPTVs sold today are HDTV-capable and feature a wide variety of audio and video inputs. You can find RPTVs ranging from 42'' to 70'' in size, from manufacturers like Hitachi, Mitsubishi, Panasonic, Samsung, and Sony; pick the model that best fits your individual viewing needs.

How CRT Rear Projection TVs Work

5 The final image shines onto the television's screen, where it is seen by the viewer. The viewer sees the combined full-color picture from the three different-colored CRTs.

4 The picture is bounced off the reflecting mirror toward the front of the rear projection set.

Projected image

1 The first rear projection televisions used CRT technology to create their pictures, and that technology remains popular today. The picture starts with a traditional video generation circuit that separates the video signal into three colors—red, green, and blue. In a traditional direct-view display, the three color signals would be used to create three electron beams within a single CRT. In a projection set, the three signals are sent to three separate CRTs, one for each primary color.

3 CRTs and focusing lens

Video circuit board

Converging the Picture

Light from the red, blue, and green CRTs combine (converge) to create white. The CRTs must be converged across all points of the screen, which can sometimes be a little tricky. To properly converge a projection set, you have to display a set of cross-hatch lines onscreen and then use the set's service controls to adjust the red/blue/green settings across all the lines. It's possible to have a set converged properly in the center of the screen, yet be off convergence in one or more corners. The process is necessary, however, because a misconverged picture will display green or red or blue fringing around the edges of objects.

3 The three CRTs are aimed at a reflecting mirror, typically located toward the bottom of the set. Proper alignment of each CRT is important because the three colors have to converge to produce a perfect white dot or line without halos or color fringing.

Reflected image

Side view

Projected image

2 The picture is displayed on three small CRTs, 5", 7" or 9" in diameter. (Larger-diameter CRTs are necessary for creating true high-definition pictures.) The red CRT displays only the red content of the picture; the green CRT displays only the green content; and the blue CRT displays only the blue content. Attached to each CRT is a lens that helps to focus the picture, and each CRT is configured to provide maximum brightness.

Mirror

How DLP Rear Projection TVs Work

1 Digital light processing (DLP) rear projection televisions are remarkably small and lightweight, thanks to the compact sizes of the optical and electronic components. The DLP system starts with the light generated by a high-performance projector lamp. Today's projector lamps have a life of 4,000 hours or more. When they wear out, they're user-replaceable and relatively inexpensive.

High-wattage long-life bulb

Rotating color wheel

Condensing lens

3 The light now shines through a rotating color wheel. The wheel is composed of red, green, and blue segments and spins rapidly to sequentially generate 16.7 million colors. (Some newer color wheels offer additional color segments and spin at a faster rate—both of which help to reduce the rainbow effect some viewers see with DLP projectors.)

2 The light from the lamp is projected through a condensing lens, which concentrates the light into a small point.

Shaping lens

Microscopic mirrors sit on top of tiny electromechanical pivots that physically tilt the mirrors to direct the flow of light and color.

4 The colored light now shines through a shaping lens, which targets the digital micromirror device.

5 The digital micromirror device (DMD) is an array of hundreds of thousands of tiny, independently hinged mirrors. There is one micromirror for each pixel in the display, all controlled by the DMD's computer processor. When the processor sends an electrical impulse to a micromirror, the mirror tilts either +10° (on) or –10° (off). (Some DMDs employ an even greater degree of tilt.) A micromirror tilted in the on position reflects light to the monitor screen; a mirror in the off position reflects no light, thus showing a black pixel onscreen. The DMD's processor coordinates the on mirrors with the colors generated by the color wheel, and our eyes blend the rapidly alternating flashes of color and see the intended hue.

Projected image

7 The final image shines onto the television's screen, where it is seen by the viewer. A typical single-chip DMD generates a picture composed of 1280 × 720 pixels (almost a million total pixels), perfect for high-definition viewing.

Projection lens

6 Light reflected off the DMD's micromirrors shines through a projection lens. This lens increases the size of the projected image.

DLP/DMD chip

How LCD Rear Projection TVs Work

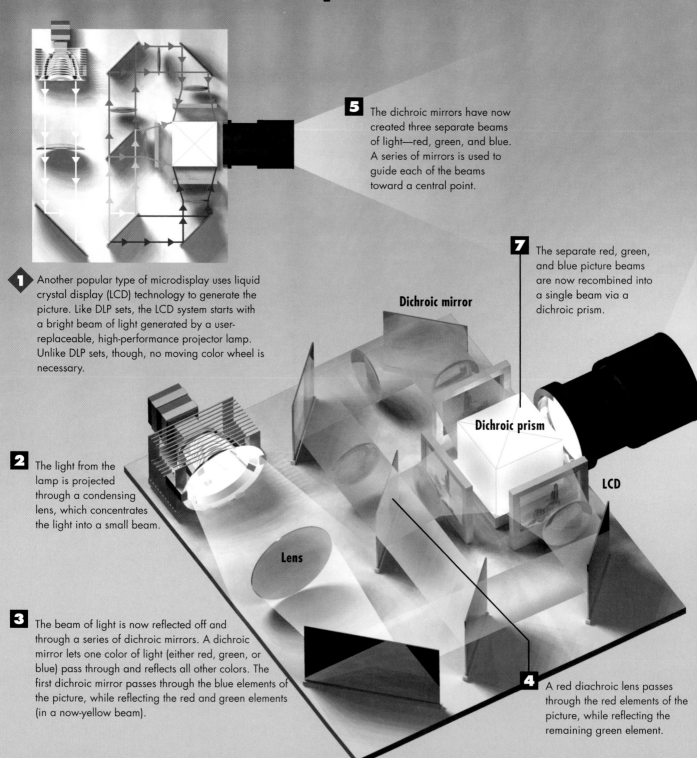

5 The dichroic mirrors have now created three separate beams of light—red, green, and blue. A series of mirrors is used to guide each of the beams toward a central point.

7 The separate red, green, and blue picture beams are now recombined into a single beam via a dichroic prism.

Dichroic mirror

Dichroic prism

LCD

1 Another popular type of microdisplay uses liquid crystal display (LCD) technology to generate the picture. Like DLP sets, the LCD system starts with a bright beam of light generated by a user-replaceable, high-performance projector lamp. Unlike DLP sets, though, no moving color wheel is necessary.

2 The light from the lamp is projected through a condensing lens, which concentrates the light into a small beam.

Lens

3 The beam of light is now reflected off and through a series of dichroic mirrors. A dichroic mirror lets one color of light (either red, green, or blue) pass through and reflects all other colors. The first dichroic mirror passes through the blue elements of the picture, while reflecting the red and green elements (in a now-yellow beam).

4 A red diachroic lens passes through the red elements of the picture, while reflecting the remaining green element.

Projected image

8 The final image is passed through an enlarging lens and shined onto the television's screen, where it is seen by the viewer. The resolution of the picture is determined by the number of pixels used in each LCD chip.

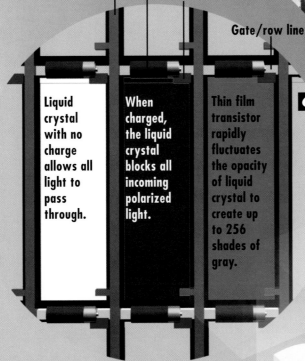

Data/column line

Capacitor

Thin film transistor

Gate/row line

Liquid crystal with no charge allows all light to pass through.

When charged, the liquid crystal blocks all incoming polarized light.

Thin film transistor rapidly fluctuates the opacity of liquid crystal to create up to 256 shades of gray.

6 Each colored beam passes through a separate LCD chip. Each chip consists of a layer of liquid crystal material sandwiched between two plates of glass. The hundreds of thousands of liquid crystals are arranged in a grid pattern, representing picture pixels. When an electric charge is applied to the chip, individual crystals rotate the plane of polarized light, effectively acting as an on/off switch for each pixel of the picture. The colored light beam passes through the LCD chip to create the screen image.

Polarizing filter blocks light.

Charged liquid crystal twists incoming light 90°.

Polarized light

How LCoS Rear Projection TVs Work

No Screen Doors
In an LCD, the wiring is fit into the spaces between the pixels, which results in wide gaps and the possibility of a "screen door" effect. In an LCoS, the wiring fits behind the glass backpane. This results in more tightly spaced pixels, with less-prominent gaps between the pixels—and no "screen door" effect.

1 Liquid crystal on silicone (LCoS) is an emerging technology that is similar to the older LCD projection technology but is capable of producing a smoother, more cinematic picture than either LCD or DLP displays. (One popular type of LCoS technology is the digital image light amplifier [D-ILA] developed by JVC.) Like LCD technology, an LCoS display starts with a bright beam of light generated by a user-replaceable, high-performance projector lamp.

2 The light from the lamp is projected through a condensing lens, which concentrates the light into a small beam.

7 The separate red, green, and blue picture beams are now recombined into a single beam via a dichroic prism.

LCoS panel

Lens

Dichroic prism

High-intensity light source

Dichroic mirrors

3 The beam of light is now reflected off and through a series of dichroic mirrors that pass through a single color, while reflecting all other colors. The first dichroic mirror passes through the blue elements of the picture, while reflecting the red and green elements (in a now-yellow beam).

4 A red diachroic lens passes through the red elements of the picture, while reflecting the remaining green element.

5 The dichroic mirrors have now created three separate beams of light—red, green, and blue. A series of mirrors is used to guide each of the beams toward individual LCoS chips.

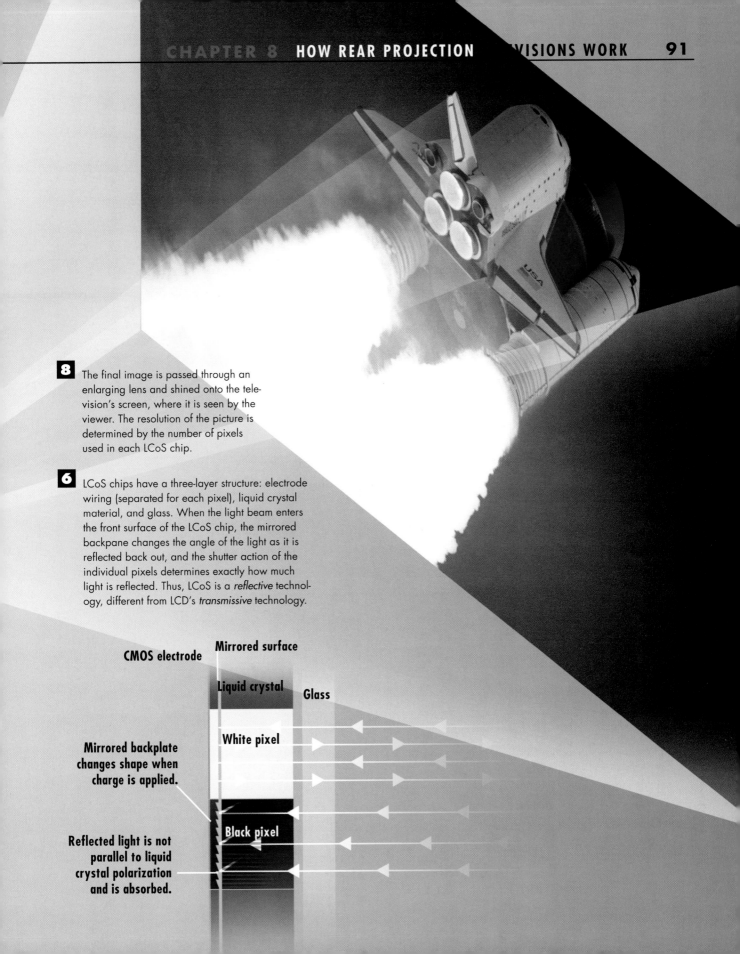

8 The final image is passed through an enlarging lens and shined onto the television's screen, where it is seen by the viewer. The resolution of the picture is determined by the number of pixels used in each LCoS chip.

6 LCoS chips have a three-layer structure: electrode wiring (separated for each pixel), liquid crystal material, and glass. When the light beam enters the front surface of the LCoS chip, the mirrored backpane changes the angle of the light as it is reflected back out, and the shutter action of the individual pixels determines exactly how much light is reflected. Thus, LCoS is a *reflective* technology, different from LCD's *transmissive* technology.

CMOS electrode

Mirrored surface

Liquid crystal

Glass

White pixel

Mirrored backplate changes shape when charge is applied.

Black pixel

Reflected light is not parallel to liquid crystal polarization and is absorbed.

CHAPTER

9

How Front Projection Televisions Work

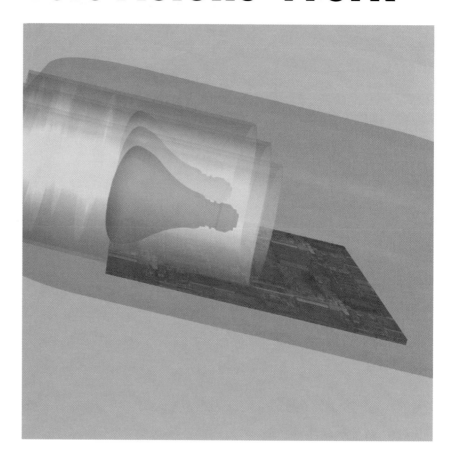

IF your home theater system dictates a very large screen (80" or larger), you have a single display choice: front projection.

A front projection television (FPTV) is a two-piece system, utilizing both a projector and a screen. The projector unit is positioned several feet in front of the large fabric screen, behind or to the side of the audience. Images are projected from the projector unit onto the screen, much the same way a movie projector displays images on a movie screen.

The size of the picture in a front projection system depends on the size of the screen, the capabilities of the projector, and the distance between the projector and the screen. Larger displays require more advanced signal processing (such as line doublers or triplers) to eliminate visible scan lines in the picture.

Today's front projectors can be driven by a variety of technologies. High-end systems typically use three small CRTs (one each for the red, green, and blue components of the picture) to create the image. Lower-priced units use either digital light projection (DLP) or liquid crystal display (LCD) microdisplay technology. CRT-based projectors produce higher-resolution pictures, but at a higher price; microdisplay-based projectors produce a brighter picture from a smaller unit—and at a lower price.

In an FPTV system, the projector unit can sit on the floor (on a stand) or be mounted on the ceiling; wherever it is, it needs to be carefully installed and calibrated for the best picture. Front projection systems are tricky to set up and typically require professional installation. They also require separate television tuners and sound systems because there's not much extra built in to the projection unit itself.

The main advantages of front projection are size and the capability to deliver on a true theater experience; if you need a super-large picture, this is literally the only way to go. FPTV's disadvantages are numerous—you need a dark room, you must have a narrow viewing angle, you might need to use the services of a professional installer, and it's costly. Entry-level FPTVs are priced similarly to high-end RPTVs, but prices on higher-end FPTVs can get into five figures and higher.

How CRT Front Projection TVs Work

4 On the screen, the three separate red, green, and blue images converge to form a single full-color image.

Projected image

Projected images can be up to 20 feet!

5 The size of the image depends on the distance of the projector to the screen. The greater the distance, the larger the projected image. Some front projection home theater systems display images up to 20 feet wide!

20" diagonal CRT TV

1 A CRT projector uses three separate CRTs, one each for red, green, and blue images. These CRTs are much smaller than the type found in direct-view televisions; 7" and 9" diameter sizes are common.

2 Each CRT is fitted with a projection lens that magnifies and projects the image coming from the picture tube. These lenses also work to correct the keystone distortion inherent in projecting a picture on a surface that is not perfectly perpendicular to the CRT projectors.

3 The three beams of colored light are projected across the room onto a separate screen.

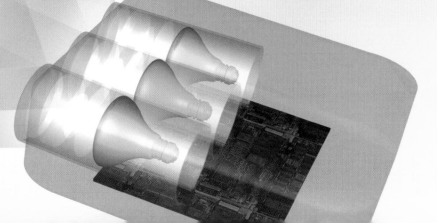

How Microdisplay Front Projection TVs Work

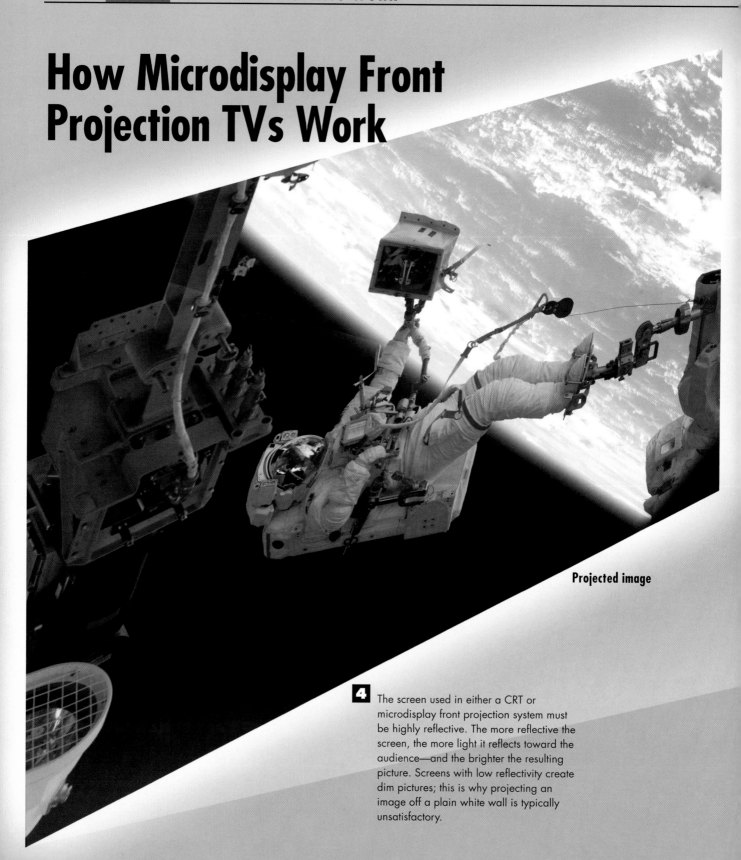

Projected image

4 The screen used in either a CRT or microdisplay front projection system must be highly reflective. The more reflective the screen, the more light it reflects toward the audience—and the brighter the resulting picture. Screens with low reflectivity create dim pictures; this is why projecting an image off a plain white wall is typically unsatisfactory.

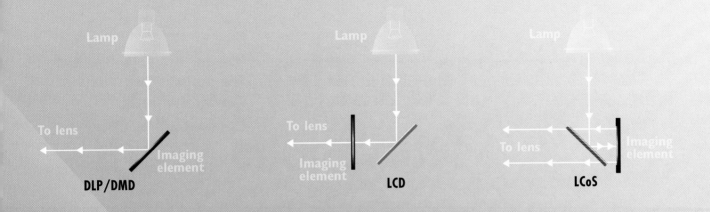

DLP/DMD

LCD

LCoS

1 A microdisplay front projection system works similarly to a CRT-based system, but with a different type of light source. In a microdisplay system, the light source can be based on DLP, LCD, or LCoS technology. The DLP/LCD/LCoS unit must be driven by a high-performance lamp to best project the image over long distances.

2 The transmitted or reflected full-color image is shone through a single projection lens, which magnifies and projects the image.

3 The beam of light is projected across the room onto a separate screen. The entire process is much like that used in the type of film projector used in movie theaters, but with modern microdisplay technology.

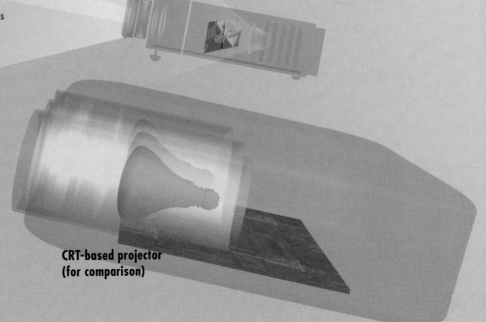

CRT-based projector (for comparison)

CHAPTER

10

How Flat-panel Televisions Work

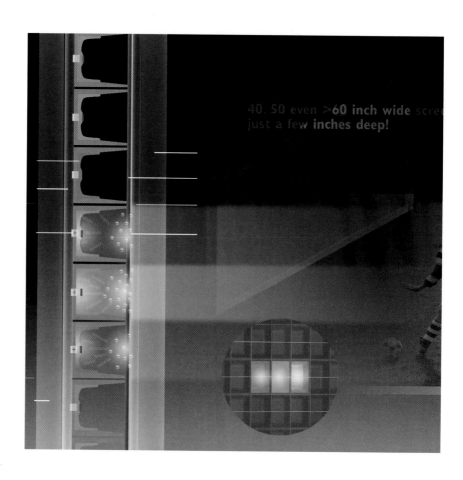

40, 50 even >60 inch wide scree
just a few inches deep!

WHEN you have little or no floor space for a big-screen TV—but plenty of spare walls—then it's time to turn to the latest video display technology: flat-panel displays. These displays, utilizing either LCD or plasma technology, are thin (6" deep or less) and can be hung on a wall or even the ceiling. It's like hanging an oil painting, except you're hanging a high-resolution video display!

Flat-panel displays are so thin because they contain no picture tubes or projection devices. Plasma displays contain glass, gas, and electrodes in a thin sandwich; LCD displays, like the ones used in laptop PCs, are made from millions of tiny liquid crystals, sandwiched between thin layers of glass or plastic.

The result, for both technologies, is a thin, lightweight (anywhere from 75 to 100 pounds, on average), high-resolution display device that can display normal television signals, HDTV programming (in full 16:9 format, with many models), and signals from personal computers. Plasma displays tend to be a little brighter than LCD displays, with blacker blacks and more vivid colors. LCD displays, on the other hand, weigh less and use less energy than plasma displays.

In addition, LCD displays don't suffer from the burn-in effect that plagues plasma displays. If you leave a static picture onscreen too long, that image will burn into the plasma display, remaining ghostly visible while watching other programs in the future. (This makes plasma a poor choice for watching letterboxed or windowpaned programming.) Burn-in isn't a problem with LCD displays.

Both types of flat-panel displays are experiencing huge surges in popularity. Today, LCD displays are best for smaller picture sizes (40" or smaller), while plasma displays are best for larger displays (42" or larger). Larger LCD displays are on their way but are currently higher-priced than similar plasma displays; smaller plasma displays aren't technically feasible.

How Plasma TVs Work

1 A plasma display works by sandwiching a layer of ionized xenon and neon gas between two thin layers of glass. The gas is contained in hundreds of thousands of tiny cells.

3 Each of the glass layers of the displays is covered with electrodes. The *address electrodes* sit behind the gas cells, along the rear glass plate. The transparent *display electrodes* (surrounded by an insulating dialectic material) are mounted above the cell, along the front glass plate. The address electrodes are arranged in vertical columns and the display electrodes are arranged in horizontal rows, creating a basic grid of individual groups of three subpixels—red, blue, and green.

4 When voltage is applied to a pair of address and display electrodes, an electric current flows through the gas in the cell. This excites, or *ionizes*, the gas, which releases ultraviolet photons.

Top view of gas plasma cells

Phosphor coating

Dialectric layer

Address electrode

A single pixel

Rear glass

Each cell is filled with xenon and neon gases.

Plasma

UV photons

Phosphor coating absorbs UV energy and gives off visible light photons.

40, 50 even >60 inch wide screens just a few inches deep!

Front glass

Magnesium oxide layer

Dialectric layer

Display electrode

2 Under normal conditions, the plasma gas is made up primarily of uncharged particles. However, when an electrical voltage is applied to the gas, negatively charged particles rush toward the positively charged area of the plasma and positively charged particles rush toward the negatively charged area. The rapidly moving particles collide with each other, exciting the gas atoms in the plasma and releasing photons of energy—which we see as light.

6 When enough subpixels light up in a pattern, a picture is created. Color intensity is increased or decreased by varying the pulses of current flowing through the different cells.

5 The ultraviolet photons interact with phosphor material coated on the inside wall of the cell. The excited phosphors give off colored light, thus illuminating a single subpixel of that specific color.

Visible light photons

Front view of subpixel cell

How LCD TVs Work

1 Like a plasma display, a flat-panel LCD display uses transmissive light technology. The principle behind the technology is that certain types of crystals, suspended in a liquid, vary in brightness when heated. By changing the temperature of the liquid crystals, different levels of brightness can be displayed.

2 The process begins when light is shown through a polarizing filter with vertical slots.

3 The polarized light now shines through a layer of liquid crystal suspension sandwiched between two panels of glass substrate. This layer contains hundreds of thousands of individual picture elements (pixels). Each pixel has three subpixels with red, green, and blue color filters.

5 Electricity is generated by a series of thin film transistors (TFTs), which are tiny switching transistors arranged in a matrix on the glass substrate. When voltage is supplied to a TFT, the liquid crystal substrate receives a charge.

Charged liquid crystals are aligned.

Backlight

Polarized glass

Liquid crystal

TFT layer

Uncharged liquid crystals are twisted.

Electrode

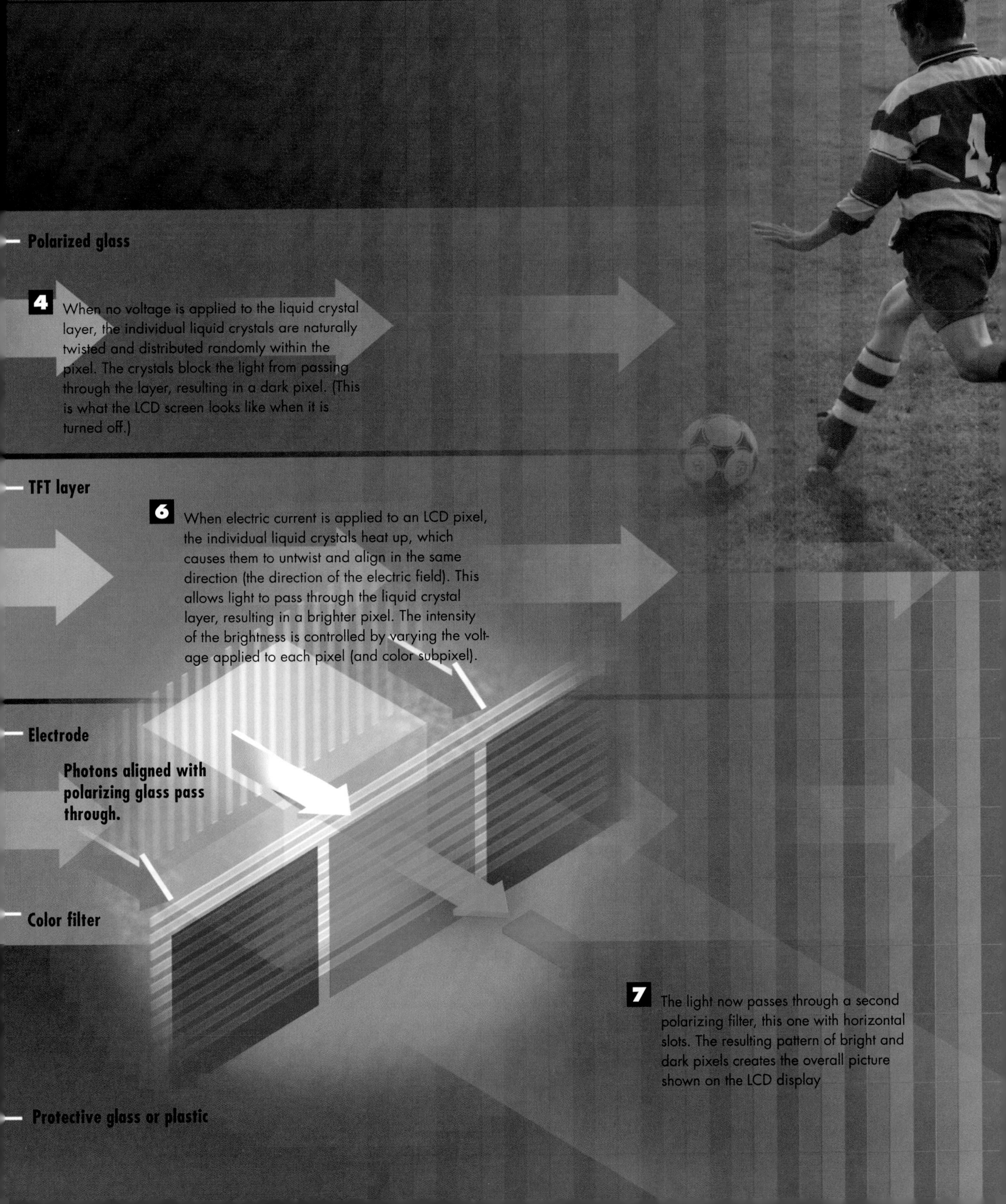

Polarized glass

4 When no voltage is applied to the liquid crystal layer, the individual liquid crystals are naturally twisted and distributed randomly within the pixel. The crystals block the light from passing through the layer, resulting in a dark pixel. (This is what the LCD screen looks like when it is turned off.)

TFT layer

6 When electric current is applied to an LCD pixel, the individual liquid crystals heat up, which causes them to untwist and align in the same direction (the direction of the electric field). This allows light to pass through the liquid crystal layer, resulting in a brighter pixel. The intensity of the brightness is controlled by varying the voltage applied to each pixel (and color subpixel).

Electrode

Photons aligned with polarizing glass pass through.

Color filter

7 The light now passes through a second polarizing filter, this one with horizontal slots. The resulting pattern of bright and dark pixels creates the overall picture shown on the LCD display

Protective glass or plastic

CHAPTER

11

How to Choose a Video Display

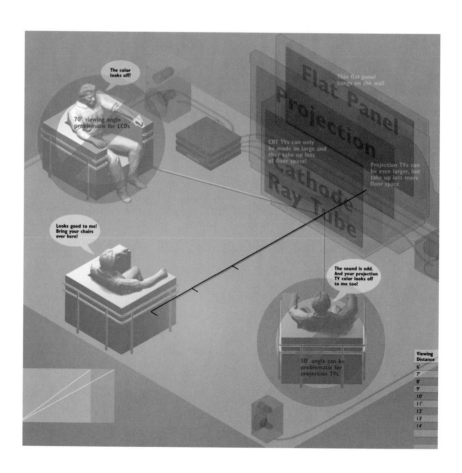

NOW that you know about all the different types of video displays available, how do you choose the right display for your own home theater system? As you can tell, it's definitely not a one-size-fits-all world.

The following pages will help guide you through this decision by comparing the pluses and minuses of each type of display. In general, however, each of the display technologies is best for specific uses:

■ **Direct-view**—Good for smaller rooms or when you're sitting only 5 or 6 feet away from the screen, when you have to deal with high ambient light levels, when you want the brightest possible picture and a wide viewing angle, or if you're on a tight budget.

■ **Rear projection**—Good if you have a larger room but want to make as few compromises as possible in terms of room lighting or viewing angle. Also a good choice if you prefer to watch movies in their original aspect ratio without worrying about screen burn-in.

■ **Front projection**—The best choice if you want the largest picture possible and the closest approximation to a movie theater experience—and don't mind restricting both viewing angle and room lighting.

■ **Flat-panel**—Good if you have little or no floor space for a television set or projector—or if you just want to show off the neat technology. Plasma flat panels are especially popular when you want a larger picture, but they present somewhat of a burn-in problem.

When choosing a set, you should also consider the number and types of video inputs on the back, the usability of the remote control, and any additional features offered (such as picture-in-picture and onscreen program guides). You should definitely get a set that's ready for HDTV broadcasts and that offers a 16:9 aspect ratio screen. And make it a point to audition each set with similar programming—not all sets using the same technology are created equal!

How Different Video Displays Compare

Direct View

Technology used: CRT

Pros:

- Excellent color and film-like picture
- Affordable

Cons:

- Big and bulky
- Limited screen sizes (40'' max.)

Rear Projection

Technologies used: CRT, DLP, LCD, LCoS

Pros:

- Self-contained units
- Large screen sizes (up to 70'')

Cons:

- Big and bulky (microprojectors less so)
- Less bright than direct view sets

Front Projection

Technologies used: CRT, DLP, LCD

Pros:

- One size fits all (variable picture size)
- Capable of extra-large pictures (100'' or more)

Cons:

- Low light output requires a darkened room
- Requires special screen for best performance

Flat-panel

Technologies used: LCD and plasma

Pros:

- Thin and wall-mountable
- Easy to place in almost any room

Cons:

- Expensive
- Not all models are true HDTV; beware lower-priced EDTV models

Display Type	Technology	Current Screen Sizes	Thickness
Direct view	CRT	5''–40''	20''–25''
Rear projection	CRT	42''–65''	22''–28''
	DLP	48''–62''	15''–20''
	LCD	42''–70''	15''–20''
	LCoS	52''–70''	16''–22''
Front projection	CRT	70''+	N/A
	DLP	70''+	N/A
	LCD	70''+	N/A
Flat-panel	LCD	13''–50''	4''–5''
	Plasma	32''–61''	4''–5''

Viewing Angle (Off center)	Contrast Ratio and Black Level	Potential for Screen Burn-in	Pros	Cons
85°	Excellent	Moderate	Best picture quality of all display types. Lowest-priced technology.	Screen size limited. Big and heavy.
30°–45°	Very good	Moderate	Lowest-priced RPTV sets. Film-like picture.	Big and bulky. Less light output than other RPTVs. Three CRTs require convergence.
75°	Good	None	Brightest picture of all RPTVs. Excellent blacks and shadow details. More compact technology than CRT projectors. Some high-end models offer 1980 × 1080 native resolution.	Moving parts (color wheel). Some viewers sensitive to "rainbows." Lamp replacement.
60°–65°	Moderate–good	None	No "rainbows" or burn-in. Good brightness and color reproduction. More compact technology than CRT projectors.	Limited contrast and black level. Possible "screen door" effects. Lamp replacement.
80°	Good	None	First RPTV technology to offer 1980 × 1080 native resolution. No "rainbows" or burn-in. Smoother, more cinematic picture than DLP or LCD projectors.	Not widely adopted. Expensive. Lamp replacement.
50°–90° (dependent on type of screen)	Very good	Moderate	Film-like picture. Highest-resolution display (w/ 9'' CRTs). Best suited for high-end professional installations.	Low light output requires a darkened room. Three CRTs require convergence.
50°–90° (dependent on type of screen)	Good	None	Extremely affordable. Brightest FPTV picture. Small projector size.	Moving parts (color wheel). Some viewers sensitive to "rainbows." Lamp replacement.
50°–90° (dependent on type of screen)	Moderate–good	None	No "rainbows." Brighter than CRT projectors. Small projector size.	Limited contrast and black level. Possible "screen door" effects. Lamp replacement.
70°–85°	Good	None	Weighs less and uses less energy than plasma. Wall mountable. No burn-in.	Vulnerable to "motion smear." Expensive, especially at larger screen sizes. Limited contrast and black level.
80°	Very good	High	Closest picture to that of traditional CRT. Excellent off-axis viewing. Wall-mountable.	Vulnerable to burn-in. Glass panel is fragile. Expensive.

How to Choose the Right Screen Size for Your Room

1 Bigger isn't always better. If the screen is too big, picture flaws (including interlace lines and the LCD "screen door" effect) will be more noticeable. The optimal screen size depends on how far away from the screen you'll be sitting, as well as which video sources you're using. For analog cable or standard definition broadcast signals shown on a 4:3 ratio display, the ideal screen size is 4" times the number of feet between you and the screen. For high definition broadcasts shown on a 16:9 ratio display, the ideal screen size is 6" times the number of feet between you and the screen. So, for example, if you're watching high-definition programming and sitting 10' from the screen, the ideal screen size is approximately 60" (6" × 10').

The color looks off?

70° viewing angle problematic for LCDs

2 Also consider how far off-axis various chairs are in your viewing room. If you're sitting too far off-axis, consider getting a slightly bigger screen or a technology with good off-axis viewing characteristics (direct-view CRT or plasma) and avoiding those technologies with poor off-axis viewing (CRT rear projection and all front projection systems).

Looks good to me! Bring your chairs over here!

4 Screen size is also dependent on the aspect ratio of the screen. Because screen size is measured diagonally, a 36" 16:9 screen will actually be a little shorter, top-to-bottom, than a 36" 4:3 screen. So, if you're moving from a traditional 4:3 ratio set to a 16:9 model, you'll need a screen that measures about 25% wider (diagonally) to maintain the same screen area for 4:3 programming.

Picture quality and audio fidelity "sweet spot."

36" diagonal 4:3 TV

36" diagonal 16:9 TV

16:9 TV approx 25% larger diagonally

3 Another practical consideration is the total size of your room; some rooms simply don't have the space for larger sets. In smaller rooms, consider a flat-panel display that will take up minimal (or no) floor space.

Thin flat panel hangs on the wall

CRT TVs can only be made so large and they take up lots of floor space!

Projection TVs can be even larger, but take up lots more floor space

The sound is odd. And your projection TV color looks off to me too!

50° angle can be problematic for projection TVs

Viewing Distance	Ideal 4:3 SDTV Screen Size	Ideal 16:9 HDTV Screen Size
6'	24" diagonal	36" diagonal
7'	28" diagonal	42" diagonal
8'	32" diagonal	48" diagonal
9'	36" diagonal	54" diagonal
10'	40" diagonal	60" diagonal
11'	44" diagonal (not available)	66" diagonal
12'	48" diagonal (not available)	72" diagonal

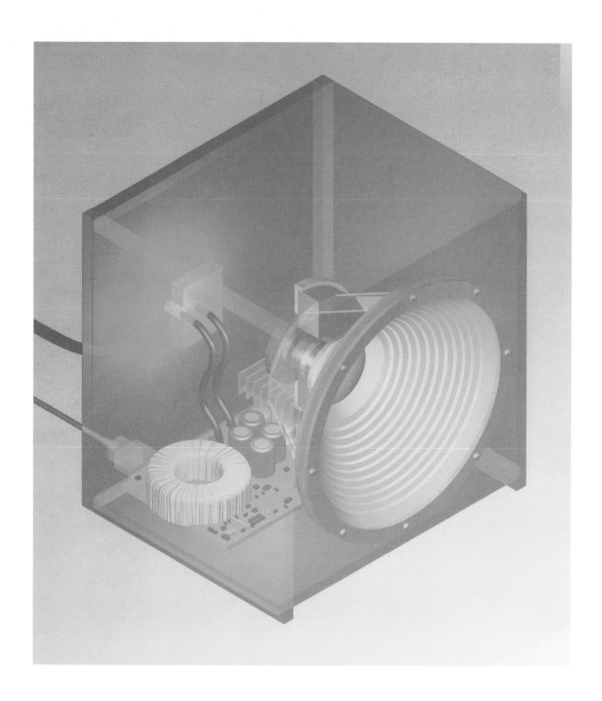

P A R T

4

HOW AUDIO WORKS

TO many consumers, the phrase *home theater system* really means *widescreen television*. While a big TV (with HDTV capability) is certainly the visual centerpiece of a home theater, the full theater experience depends as much on sound as it does on picture. To that end, it's important to pay as much attention to the audio components in your system as to the video display.

Home audio systems have been around a lot longer than home video systems. The original home audio system was a simple single-speaker AM radio; today's home audio systems are more likely to include multiple audio sources and multiple speakers. (And, yes, most systems today can still receive those primitive low-fidelity AM signals.)

Audio is important not just for listening to music, but also for watching big-screen movies. Virtually all movies made over the past decade or so utilize surround sound, which places the soundtrack all around the listener. Dialogue comes from the front of the room, special effects come from behind, and music fills the entire listening space. This is especially noticeable in special-effects–laden action/adventure films; *Lord of the Rings* is a lot more impressive on a good surround-sound system than it is on a single-speaker television set.

To fill your home theater room with sound, you need the right equipment—and the right technology. It all starts with a component called an *audio/video receiver*, which functions as the control center of your entire system. Most A/V receivers let you connect all your audio and video components and then switch between inputs with a single remote control. You connect your CD player, DVD player, digital video recorder, and cable/satellite box to the inputs of your A/V receiver and then connect the output of the A/V receiver to your video display. Whatever you select on the receiver's remote appears on the television screen.

The A/V receiver also serves as the main processor/amplifier for your system's audio. Surround-sound sources (either broadcast or DVD) are fed into the receiver, which decodes the surround-sound signal using the appropriate technology. Most soundtracks today are encoded with Dolby Digital surround sound, which feeds the audio to six separate speakers—three in the front of the room, two in the back, and a final subwoofer for the deep bass signals. Pop in a DVD with a Dolby Digital soundtrack, and your A/V receiver will create room-filling sound.

Of course, the sound you hear is strongly affected by the speakers you use. Some consumers prefer small, unobtrusive bookshelf speakers that can be easily placed in any living room. Others prefer larger floor-standing speakers that are better for reproducing music. (Remember, your home theater system will also function as your main music system, so music CDs are every bit as important as movie soundtracks.) Whichever type of speaker system you choose, the main sound will be supplemented by a separate subwoofer, which reproduces the very lowest bass frequencies; you need a good sub to hear all the rumbles and explosions in action/adventure films.

When you're budgeting for a new home theater system, you should actually spend more money on the audio components than you do on the video display. Figure spending a third of your budget on the television set, a third on speakers, and a third on the A/V receiver and other source components (such as a DVD player). As with all electronic devices, the bigger your budget, the better the components you can get—in terms of both functionality and sound quality.

Shopping for audio components requires careful listening. You should always test drive receivers and (especially) speakers before you buy; specifications alone aren't a good barometer of how a system will actually sound. A higher-powered receiver might not sound as good as a lower-powered one, nor do bigger speakers always sound better than smaller ones. Specs are important, but they don't tell the whole story.

And here's something that might surprise you: As impressive as a slam-bang surround sound movie soundtrack might sound, movie audio is actually much less demanding for a system than music audio. That's because, despite the deep bass and loud explosions, the dynamic range of a movie soundtrack is less than that of a good music CD. Your favorite DVD might be loud, but it really isn't that impressive from a pure audio standpoint.

Reproducing music—especially acoustic music—is much more demanding. A high-quality music CD has a very wide dynamic range, meaning that the soft passages are very soft and the loud passages are very loud. In addition, music uses a full range of frequencies (from the lowest bass notes to the highest highs of a cymbal), whereas movie sound effects are typically limited to a small frequency range. The proof is in the listening; most DVD soundtracks sound good on even moderately priced audio systems, but music CDs require high-fidelity audio systems to achieve their full sonic potential.

Don't rely on the source material in the showroom, either; take your own DVDs and CDs to try the components you're interested in. (It's important to use material that you're familiar with, so you'll know how it *should* sound.) And when in doubt, go by weight; for some reason, the best audio components are almost always the heaviest!

CHAPTER

12

How Audio Equipment Works

THE processing of the audio signals in a home theater system is just as important as the processing of the video signals. This audio processing is typically done by a single component, called an *audio/video receiver*. An A/V receiver combines the functions of three separate components—a preamplifier, power amplifier, and surround sound processor.

A/V receivers are available at a variety of price points, from under $200 to more than $6,000. While all A/V receivers perform similar functions, the price differential comes from varying control capabilities and sound quality. Consider the following variables:

- **Power**—In general, you're better off getting as much power as you can afford, within limits. Don't sweat differences of 10–20 watts per channel between models because the difference won't likely be noticeable. However, do look beyond simple power ratings to compare total harmonic distortion levels—which typically have more effect on the actual sound than do power ratings. A heavier unit often indicates a more powerful unit.

- **Inputs and outputs**—This is key. Make sure there are enough—and the right kinds of—input and output jacks to connect all your components. Also look for at least one front-panel audio/video connection for camcorder and videogame use.

- **Control**—You operate an A/V receiver with its remote control unit, and there are big differences in remote controls. Look for a unit that feels right to you and is easy for others to figure out and use. Also look for a universal or learning remote that can be programmed to control all the components in your home theater system.

- **Surround processing**—Almost all A/V receivers today decode both Dolby Digital and Dolby Pro Logic sources. If you want a system with both surround and back speakers, make sure that the receiver includes a Dolby Digital EX 6.1/7.1 decoder. Also look for a built-in DTS decoder for DVDs using this alternative (and some say superior) surround format.

- **Sound quality**—Before you buy, listen. Does this model sound noticeably different or better than comparable models? Is the sound loud enough, clean enough, and smooth enough? Make sure you bring your own source material when comparing units—and compare different types of sources, both movies and music.

How Preamplifiers Work

Remote control

1 The preamplifier—whether a freestanding component or part of an audio/video receiver—is the command center for your entire home theater system. (In fact, some people refer to preamplifiers as *control amplifiers*.) Most preamplifiers today can be controlled either via front-panel buttons and knobs or via a remote control unit.

2 The first job of the preamplifier is to switch between different audio and video inputs. The preamplifier has a variety of inputs on its back panel, to which you connect all your home theater components—CD player, DVD player, and so on. The preamplifier's switching circuit lets you select a specific component as your current video or audio source.

Pre/Pros

Most home theater preamps are actually preamp/processors (sometimes called *pre/pros*) that combine traditional preamplification functions with a surround-sound processor. The advantage of having a separate pre/pro or preamp is noise and heat reduction; because the power amplifier generates both heat and electronic hum, separating the control circuitry into a separate component results in higher fidelity.

DOWN UP MODE MENU

3 The preamplifier also serves to preamplify low-level output signals from your video and audio sources up to the line level your amplifier needs to operate. Preamplifiers do not amplify signals high enough to send directly to speakers, of course; that's what an amplifier does. However, the signal level coming from a source component is not high enough to be read by the amplifier. Hence, the preamp has to triple the strength of the signal before it can be fed to the amplifier.

4 In addition to adding gain to the source signal, the preamplifier also serves as a volume control for the signal. The volume is controlled by a potentiometer connected to the low-level amplifier circuit.

Back of preamplifier

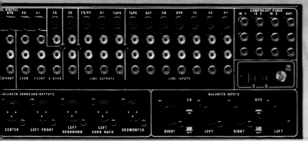

How Power Amplifiers Work

1 The job of a power amplifier is to take the low-level audio signal coming from your system's preamplifier and boost them to a level that can be sent to your system's speakers. This is done by duplicating the low-level signal in a higher-level signal, generating successively larger copies. Contrary to popular belief, an amplifier doesn't make the original signal bigger; it creates a brand-new signal from the raw AC power you supply to it. The original input signal is used only as a template for the resulting higher-level signal.

2 The low-level input signal is fed into the amplifier's input circuit, which consists of one or more bipolar transistors. Each transistor has three semiconductor layers—the emitter, base, and collector layers. The negative electrons in the input signal feed into the transistor's emitter layer.

3 Incoming alternating current (AC) power from a standard wall outlet is fed into a power transformer, which consists of several windings of insulated wire. The magnetic properties of the wire windings transform the 120-volt power down to a much lower voltage. A bridge rectifier then (consisting of four diodes in a specific orientation) converts the AC voltage into direct current (DC) power. Large capacitors are used to smooth the voltage, and the DC power is now fed into the transistor's base layer, via the base electrode.

Power transformer

4 The base layer of the transistor is positively charged, which attracts the negatively charged electrons from the emitter layer. The low-level voltage variations from the original signal in the emitter layer shape the higher-level electrical pulses in the base layer, thus recreating the original signal, but at a higher level. Thus the signal level is boosted via a duplication process.

Low-level input signal

Base electrode

Electrode	N-type material (negatively charged)	P-type material modulates the flow of electrons based on the lower-level input signal.	N-type material (negatively charged)	Electrode	Higher-level output signal
	Emitter	**Base**	**Collector**		

Heatsink

10X power = 2X volume

Raising the Volume

Small increases in power don't result in noticeable differences in loudness. To double the volume level in your system (measured in terms of sound pressure levels), you need 10 times the power—which means the volume difference between an 80-watt amplifier and a 100-watt amplifier is negligible. The bigger benefit of a high-powered amplifier is improved sound quality because more head room is available to handle sudden dynamic changes.

Clean Sound

The best amplifiers aren't just powerful; they also reproduce extremely clean sound, with very little noise or distortion. The final output signal should mimic the original signal as closely as possible, even though it has been boosted numerous times; this is measured in terms of *total harmonic distortion* (the lower the better) and *signal-to-noise ratio* (the higher the better).

Heatsink

7 Because transistors generate excess heat energy, the heat must be dissipated through a series of heatsinks. The more powerful the amplifier, the bigger the heatsinks needed. (Some installers add an external cooling fan to help dissipate heat buildup when the power amplifier is installed in an enclosed cabinet.)

5 The electrons now move through the positively charged emitter layer to the transistor's negatively charged output layer and onto the next stage of amplification. Most amplifiers have multiple stages to produce 100 or more watts of output power, with each transistor representing a single stage. The final stage of amplification feeds the now-boosted signal directly to your system's speakers.

6 A multichannel amplifier hosts one separate amplifier circuit for each channel. For example, a 5.1-channel amplifier has five separate channels of amplification. (The ".1" subwoofer contains its own amplifier—all it needs is a line-level output signal, without any additional amplification.)

How Surround-Sound Processors Work

1 A surround-sound processor is necessary to decode the incoming audio signal into multiple surround-sound channels. The surround-sound processor can be a standalone device (common in high-end professional installations) or included in either a preamplifier/processor component or an audio/video receiver.

2 Digital surround-sound signals (such as Dolby Digital and DTS) are encoded as discrete channels on a DVD or in an HDTV signal. The incoming signal is broken into blocks of 512 bits each, and these are then fed into a continuous datastream. The surround-sound processor analyzes the datastream and "unpacks" the individual blocks into continuous signals for each channel—front left, front center, front right, left surround, right surround, and the low frequency effect (LFE) channel sent to the subwoofer.

Surround sound processor

Multiple Decoders

Most surround-sound processing devices include multiple surround decoders. It's common to find digital decoders for Dolby Digital and DTS, and analog decoders for Dolby Pro Logic and DTS NEO, all in the same unit. The surround-sound processor will sense which surround format is used and pass the signal to the appropriate decoder.

**Decoder A
Dolby Digital**

Front left

Front center

Front right

Surround left

Surround right

Subwoofer

**Decoder B
Dolby Pro Logic**

3 Analog surround-sound signals (such as Dolby Pro Logic) are encoded into a matrixed stereo signal. The surround-sound processor decodes these matrixed signals and separates them into front left, front center, front right, and surround channels.

Left

Center

Right

Subwoofer

Decoder C Stereo

4 Pure two-channel stereo signals are either passed through the surround-sound processor or fed through digital signal processing (DSP) circuitry for simulated surround-sound effects. These computer-generated sound fields are used to reproduce the sound of music in various concert halls and theaters.

Left

Right

Decoder D Mono

5 In addition to the straight surround-sound decoding, the surround-sound processor also "down mixes" multiple-channel material into two-channel stereo and single-channel mono feeds for those systems without surround-sound speakers.

Mono

6 The signals for the multiple surround-sound channels are next fed into a separate preamplifier for further processing before they are boosted by the system's amplifiers (one amplifier per channel). If the signals are fed to a separate preamplifier component, a digital optical or coaxial connection is used.

How Audio/Video Receivers Work

1 For most listeners, the functions of the preamplifier, surround-sound processor, and amplifier can be combined into a single component called an audio/video (A/V) receiver. The A/V receiver functions as the central hub for your entire home theater system.

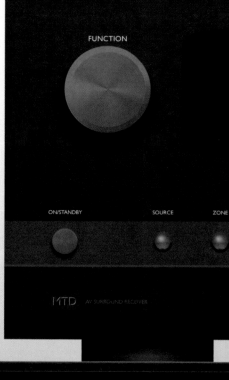

2 The typical A/V receiver contains inputs for numerous audio and video devices. It's common to find line-level audio inputs (for CD players and tape decks), digital audio inputs (for DVD players and satellite receivers), composite video inputs, S-video inputs, component video inputs, and (on some high-end models) DVI and HDMI digital video inputs.

3 The A/V receiver controls the switching between the various inputs, typically via some sort of universal remote control.

4 The signal from the selected audio input is fed to the A/V receiver's internal preamplifier.

5 Surround-sound audio signals are first fed to an internal surround-sound processor and then to the preamplifier.

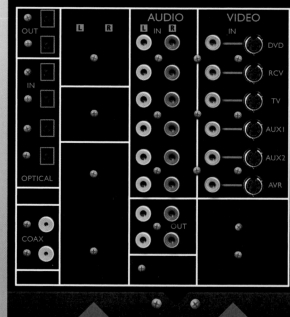

6 The signal from the preamplifier is fed to the internal amplifiers—one for each channel.

AM/FM Radio

Most audio/video receivers also include a built-in AM/FM radio receiver for receiving over-the-air radio signals.

9 Video for the selected input device is fed from the receiver's output jacks to the connected video display. Some receivers will upconvert the signal from composite and S-video inputs into higher-performance component video signals, thus facilitating a single component video connection between the receiver and video display.

8 Line-level audio for the LFE channel bypasses the internal amplifier and flows directly from the preamplifier circuit to the connected subwoofer.

7 The audio output from the amplifier is fed directly to the system's speakers. Speakers can be connected to the receiver by a variety of methods, including simple spring clips or binding posts (for either bare wire or spade lugs) and banana plugs.

13

How Speakers Work

WHILE all the components in your home theater system work together to deliver a signal to your speakers, it's your speakers that actually deliver the sound to your ears—which makes the speakers perhaps the most important component of your system.

All speaker enclosures contain one or more *drivers*. Small drivers, called *tweeters*, reproduce high frequencies (2,000Hz or higher); large drivers, called *woofers*, reproduce low frequencies (2,000Hz or below). Most speaker enclosures include at least two of these speaker drivers, although some enclosures include a third speaker, called a *midrange* driver, to better reproduce the frequencies where the tweeter and woofer meet. The circuitry used to split the signals between different drivers is called a *crossover*.

Speaker systems come in all shapes and sizes. The three primary types of speaker enclosures are

- **Floor-standing speakers**—These are speakers that are big enough to stand on the floor (either on their own or with the help of speaker stands). Floor-standing speakers typically are larger than other types of speakers; reproduce a wider range of frequencies (including deep bass); and are quite efficient, producing more volume per watt. This is the preferred design for listening to music.

- **Bookshelf speakers**—These are speakers that are small enough to fit on a typical bookshelf. Because of their reduced size, bookshelf speakers feature small woofers or, in some instances, no woofer at all. To reproduce the full range of frequencies, then, bookshelf speakers are typically supplemented by a separate subwoofer.

- **Satellite speakers**—These are very small speakers, typically containing a single tiny driver. Satellite speakers are small enough that they can be mounted or placed just about anywhere; full frequency response is accomplished by adding a separate subwoofer to the system.

In addition to these main speaker types, a subwoofer is often used to reproduce very low bass frequencies (below 200Hz). This is a speaker with its own built-in amplifier and a very large (8" or larger) driver. Today, subwoofers are standard in surround-sound systems—even those that use full-range floor-standing speakers.

How Woofers and Tweeters Work

1 Both woofers and tweeters work by converting electric signals into air movement, which is manifested as sound waves. The process starts when the amplifier section of the A/V receiver sends an electric signal to the speaker driver. This signal fluctuates between a positive and a negative charge on the red wire; the current moves one way and then reverses and flows the other way, in an *alternating current*.

3 The voice coil is positioned in a constant magnetic field created by a permanent magnet, also located at the base of the speaker. The positive end of the electromagnet is attracted to the negative pole of the permanent magnet, and the negative end of the electromagnet is repelled by the positive pole of the permanent magnet. When the electromagnet's polar orientation switches, so does the direction of repulsion and attraction; this pushes the voice coil back and forth in a rapid motion.

Tweeter

Speaker wires carry signal as AC current from the AV receiver.

Permanent magnet

Voice coil

Flexible speaker cone

2 The electric signal flows to the speaker's *voice coil*, which is actually a coil of wire wrapped around a piece of magnetic metal, such as iron. When electric current is run through the wire, this creates a magnetic field around the coil, turning the voice coil into an electromagnet. The alternating current fed to the voice coil causes the polar orientation of the electromagnet to reverse itself several times a second.

Woofer

Managing Multiple Drivers
Most speaker enclosures include both a woofer and a tweeter; for quality sound reproduction, low-frequency signals should not be sent to the smaller tweeter, nor should high-frequency signals be sent to the larger woofer. To this end, the incoming signal is first fed to a *crossover* circuit (one for each driver), composed of capacitors and inductors, which filters electric signals above a specific frequency. In a typical passive crossover design, frequencies above 2,000Hz are fed to the tweeter while frequencies below 2,000Hz are fed to the driver.

5 As the air vibrates, it forms sound waves, which travel to the listener's ears. The sound waves are shaped by the frequency and amplitude of the original electrical signal, which dictates the rate and distance that the voice coil and speaker cone move.

4 As the voice coil moves back and forth, it pushes and pulls on the attached speaker cone. (Some tweeters use a flexible metal dome instead of the traditional paper cone.) The moving cone serves as a diaphragm or air pump, vibrating the air in front of the speaker.

Cone pushes air very rapidly to create a range of audio frequencies.

How a Subwoofer Works

1 The subwoofer is responsible for reproducing the very lowest bass frequencies in music and movie soundtracks. Without a subwoofer, your home theater system will lack a strong bottom, so music will sound thin and explosions and other special effects will lack the gut-shaking punch that audiences like.

2 The signal that is fed to the subwoofer starts out as the low frequency effects (LFE) channel of a Dolby Digital or DTS 5.1-channel stream. (The LFE channel/ subwoofer is the ".1" of the system.) The LFE channel handles the low bass for all the other channels of the soundtrack (left, center, right, and surround channels) and is sent via a line-level connection from the A/V receiver to the subwoofer.

LFE signal

AC power

3 Unlike other speakers, the subwoofer is a powered speaker, which means it contains its own built-in amplifier. (Because of this, your subwoofer must be plugged into a power outlet.) The line-level input signal is fed into the power amplifier, where it is amplified by anywhere from 100 to 500 watts of power.

Amplifier

Woofer

Side-firing subwoofer

4 The amplified signal is now passed to the subwoofer's large woofer, which resonates with the signal level. Most subwoofers incorporate woofers 10''–18'' in size, capable of reproducing frequencies in the 20Hz–200Hz ranges.

Passive Subs

Some high-end subwoofers are passive speakers—that is, they don't have a built-in amplifier. Some audiophiles claim that separating the subwoofer's speaker from its electronics produces cleaner sound. A passive sub must be powered by an external amplifier, separate from the system's A/V receiver.

Sub Placement

The sound produced by a subwoofer is so low that it's nondirectional, meaning you can't tell where the sound is coming from. This enables you to place the subwoofer anywhere in your home theater room—although the best placement is typically to the front of the room, just to the left or right of the main speakers.

Amplifier

LFE signal

AC power

6 Subwoofers can be either front-firing or down-firing. A front-firing subwoofer mounts the speaker in the front or side of the cabinet, so the sound is fired directly at the listener. A down-firing subwoofer mounts the speaker on the bottom of the cabinet, so the sound is radiated downward and bounces off the floor; depending on the type of floor, this can enhance the bass frequencies. (Wood floors are best for this.) Front-firing subwoofers typically have a cleaner sound, whereas down-firing subwoofers sometimes produce a stronger sound.

Woofer

Down-firing subwoofer

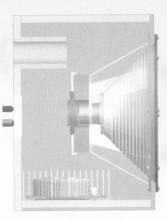

5 Most subwoofers use a sealed box design, which produces tight, well-defined bass. Other subwoofers use a ported design, in which additional bass is produced through a hole, or port, in the side of the cabinet. A ported subwoofer can typically deliver lower bass tones per watt of amplification than a similar sealed box subwoofer.

How Different Speaker Enclosures Work

Acoustic suspension

Air pressure changes within a sealed enclosure.

Bass reflex

Port in side allows air pressure to equate.

1 Speaker enclosures utilize several types of designs, each with its own acoustical properties. The most common type of design is the *acoustic suspension enclosure*, sometimes called the *sealed enclosure*. In this design, the speaker enclosure is completely sealed so that no air can escape. As the speaker drivers move in and out, they push air forward into the room and backward into the speaker enclosure. This compresses and expands the air inside the enclosure; the amplifier must boost its electrical input signal to overcome the force of this air pressure. To this end, acoustic suspension speakers are the least efficient form of speaker enclosure, generating lower sound levels per each watt of amplification. The benefit of this design is a very tight, focused sound—as well as more low bass from a smaller box.

2 Another popular type of speaker design is the *bass reflex enclosure*, sometimes called the *ported enclosure* because of its use of one or more small vents or ports. The port helps to equalize the air pressure that builds up inside the speaker enclosure; when the driver contracts inward, it pushes air backward into the enclosure, and thus out of the enclosure through the port. This design provides greater speaker efficiency, increasing the bass output of a speaker by around 3 dB, which means louder sound levels can be had with lower levels of amplification. (For example, a bass reflex speaker powered by a 100-watt amplifier generates the same sound level as an acoustic suspension speaker powered by a 200-watt amplifier.) The downside to this design is that the sound leaked through the port, generated by the backward movement of the speaker, isn't as controlled as the sound generated by a normal speaker driver. This sometimes results in less-precise sound quality; the lower frequency ranges, especially, can sound sloppy compared to other speaker designs.

Passive radiator

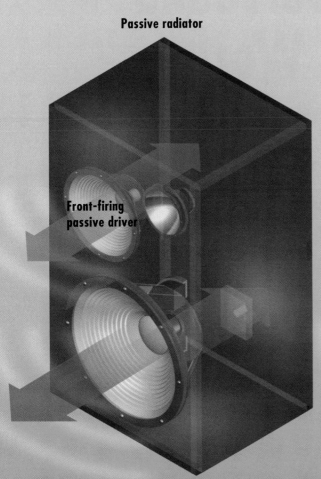

Front-firing
passive driver

Dipole

Back-projecting
passive driver

3 A *passive radiator enclosure* is similar to a bass reflex enclosure, with one notable change. Instead of venting the sound through a simple port in the cabinet, the traditional round hole is replaced by a passive driver—that is, a speaker driver that does not have a voice coil and is not connected to an amplifier. The cone of the passive driver is moved only by the sound waves generated by the speaker's active drivers, in a sympathetic fashion. The internal sound waves hit and move the cone of the passive driver, which in turn vibrates and creates its own sound waves moving forward. This reinforces the sound coming from the active drivers, which improves speaker efficiency (louder sound without increasing amplification) while maintaining the accuracy of the sound (because the enclosure is still airtight). That said, the passive radiator design is a compromise, in that it is typically neither as efficient as a ported bass reflex enclosure nor as aurally precise as a sealed acoustic suspension enclosure.

4 Some passive radiator enclosures face the active drivers in one direction and the passive drivers in the other—typically toward the back of the speaker. This type of design is called a *dipole* speaker, and it works to diffuse the sound in all directions. Because of this spreading out of the sound, some listeners like to use dipole speakers as surround speakers when listening to classical music.

CHAPTER

14

How Surround Sound Works

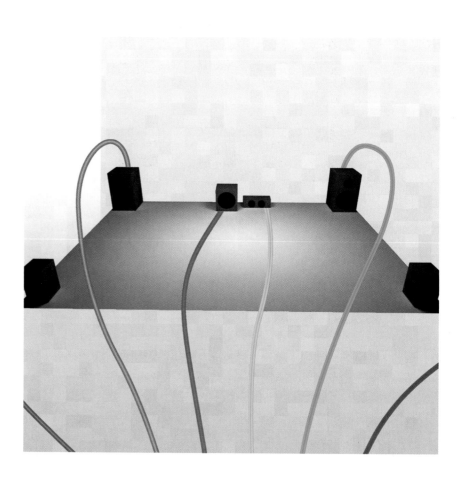

SURROUND sound for home video has been around in one form or another for more than 20 years. Today's most popular surround format is Dolby Digital, which can reproduce up to 5.1 channels of audio. The five primary channels are front left, front center (typically located just above or below the television screen), front right, left surround, and right surround. While many listeners mistakenly place their surround speakers at the rear of the room, these speakers are designed to literally surround the listener by being placed to the sides of the primary listening location, level with or just slightly behind your ears.

The ".1" part of the equation is a separate low frequency effects (LFE) channel that reproduces the very lowest bass information. This channel is fed to a powered subwoofer, which can be located anywhere within your listening space.

Some new systems include 6.1- or 7.1-channel surround technology. The sixth and seventh channels are true rear channels; these speakers should be located directly behind the listener. In a 6.1/7.1-channel system, you end up with speakers in front of you (left, center, and right front), speakers beside you (left and right surround), and speakers behind you (left and right rear). With this setup, you're literally surrounded by sound; you're put in the middle of a movie soundtrack, with gunshots, explosions, and other special effects whizzing past your head, all around the room.

All surround-sound technologies encode the audio information on the movie's normal soundtrack. Older technologies (such as Dolby Pro Logic) "hid" the rear-channel information within the front-channel information, using matrixing algorithms to mix the different channels together for storage or transmission and then separating the information on playback. Newer technologies (such as Dolby Digital and DTS) dedicate discrete data tracks for each channel of information, thus providing more precise positioning and eliminating channel leakage. (Although, just to be confusing, one of the newest formats—Dolby Digital EX —adds rear channels that are matrixed within the discrete left and right surround channel information.)

Two companies compete in the home surround sound market. The market leader is Dolby Laboratories, with its popular Dolby Digital, Dolby Digital EX, Dolby Pro Logic, and Dolby Pro Logic IIx formats. Dolby competes with Digital Theater Systems, with its similar DTS, DTS ES, and DTS Neo:6 formats. Most DVDs come encoded with Dolby Digital soundtracks, although some support DTS; the new HDTV broadcast standard mandates Dolby Digital soundtracks.

Two surround sound formats, Dolby Pro Logic IIx and DTS Neo:6, are specially designed to simulate surround sound from standard two-channel programming, such as music CDs and video games. Computer technology is used to analyze the original audio and create pseudo-surround effects; the results are variable, as you might expect, but often surprisingly realistic!

Technology marches on, of course, and Dolby Laboratories and Digital Theater Systems have introduced even newer formats to take advantage of the increased bandwidth promised by the upcoming generation of high-definition DVDs. Dolby Digital Plus offers 7.1 discrete channels at a higher bit rate than normal Dolby Digital; Dolby TrueHD offers lossless encoding for even better fidelity; and DTS HD offers both lossless encoding and an unlimited number of surround channels. The best is yet to come!

How Dolby Digital Works

Front left

Center

Front right

Left
surround

Right
surround

1 The Dolby Digital system incorporates five discrete channels of sound, plus a separate low frequency effects (LFE) channel, in a 5.1-channel configuration. The five channels (front left, front center, front right, left surround, and right surround) are originally recorded and mixed by the programming's sound engineers to create an enveloping sound field. In most instances, the center channel is used for primary dialogue, the front left and right speakers for music and offcenter dialogue, and the surround channels for sound effects and reverberation.

**<200MHz
low-frequency
effects**

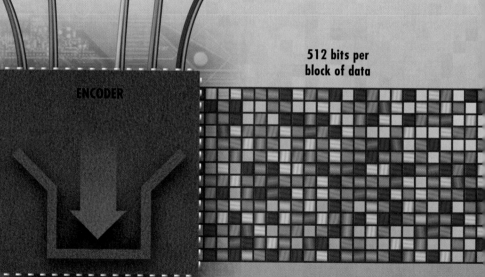

**512 bits per
block of data**

ENCODER

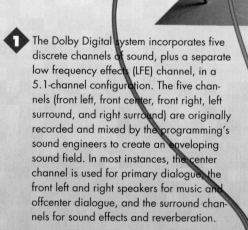

2 The original analog recording is converted to five distinct audio channels; all frequencies below 200Hz are sliced off and fed to a separate LFE channel. These analog channels are then converted into corresponding digital data streams. (Note that a Dolby Digital recording doesn't have to include all 5.1 channels; some Dolby Digital soundtracks have 2.1 or 2.0 or even 1.0 channels, depending on the source material.)

3 The six digital audio channels are passed through a Dolby Digital encoder, which breaks each channel into small blocks of 512 bits each. These blocks of data are then mixed into a continuous digital data stream.

DTS Versus Dolby Digital

DTS—which stands for Digital Theater Sound—is a 5.1-channel surround sound alternative to Dolby Digital. DTS differs from Dolby Digital in that it uses less compression to store its signals—a 3:1 compression scheme as opposed to Dolby Digital's 12:1 compression. This results in slightly better sound; unfortunately, far fewer DVDs are available with DTS soundtracks than there are that use Dolby Digital.

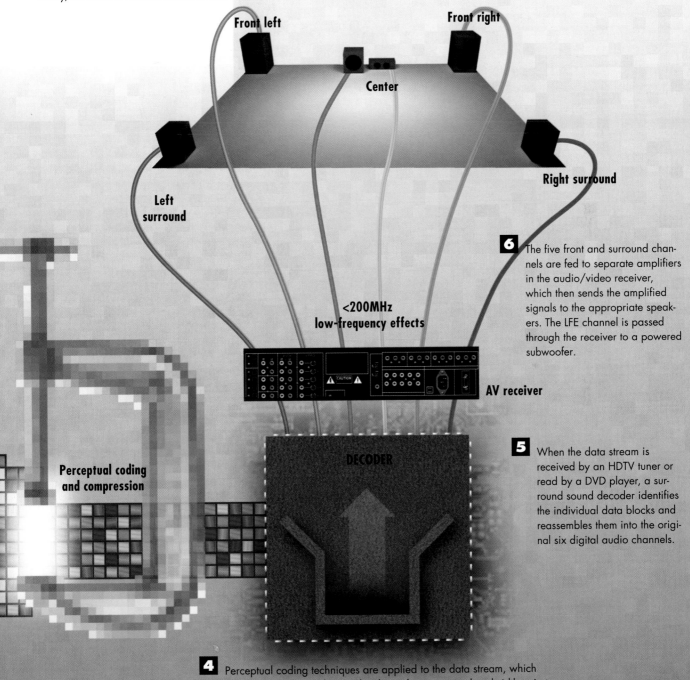

Front left

Front right

Center

Right surround

Left surround

6 The five front and surround channels are fed to separate amplifiers in the audio/video receiver, which then sends the amplified signals to the appropriate speakers. The LFE channel is passed through the receiver to a powered subwoofer.

<200MHz low-frequency effects

AV receiver

Perceptual coding and compression

DECODER

5 When the data stream is received by an HDTV tuner or read by a DVD player, a surround sound decoder identifies the individual data blocks and reassembles them into the original six digital audio channels.

4 Perceptual coding techniques are applied to the data stream, which eliminates duplicate data and reduces the necessary bandwidth to just 1/12 of the original. The compressed data stream is now encoded onto a DVD disc or transmitted as part of an HDTV broadcast.

How 6.1- and 7.1-Channel Surround Sound Works

Front left

Center

Front right

Surround right

Surround left

Rear left

Rear right

1 The most popular 6.1/7.1-channel system is Dolby Digital EX. In this system, the five front and surround channels are created and managed the same as they are in a traditional Dolby Digital 5.1-channel system, as is the LFE channel.

Dolby Digital EX

ENCODER

2 The information for the single rear channel (in a 6.1-channel soundtrack) or the left rear channel (in a 7.1-channel soundtrack) is reduced by 3dB and then mixed equally into the data streams for the left and right surround channels.

3 In a 7.1-channel soundtrack, the information for the right rear channel is reduced by 3dB and then mixed equally into the data streams for left and right surround channels. Each half of the signal gets a 90° phase shift, with the result that the rear channel data mixed into the left surround channel is 180° out of phase with the rear channel data mixed into the right surround channel.

<200MHz LFE

4 When the Dolby Digital EX data stream is decoded, the data that is identical in the left and right surround channels is identified and separated into a new single rear (for 6.1-channel soundtracks) or left rear (for 7.1-channel soundtracks) channel. The signal is then boosted by 3dB to compensate for the original 3dB level reduction.

Left and right rear are mixed together with the left and right surround.

DECODER

5 For 7.1-channel soundtracks, the decoder now identifies the data that is different between the left and right surround channels and separates it into a new right rear channel. The data from each channel receives a 90° phase shift to put the data in phase with itself. It also receives a 3dB level boost to compensate for the original level reduction.

6 All the individual channels (front left, front center, front right, left surround, right surround, left rear, and right rear) are now fed to the appropriate amplifiers. The LFE channel is passed through the receiver to a powered subwoofer.

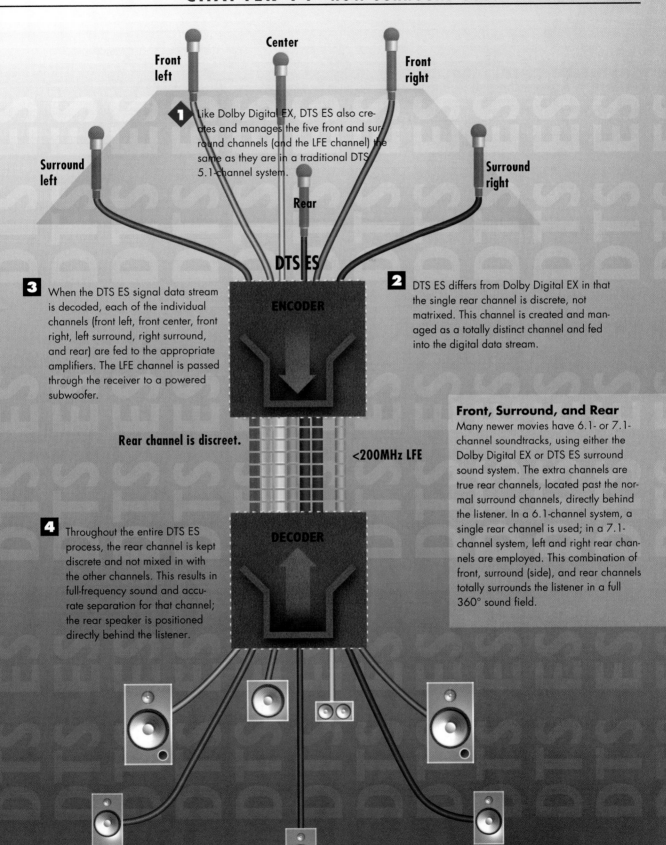

Center

Front left

Front right

1 Like Dolby Digital EX, DTS ES also creates and manages the five front and surround channels (and the LFE channel) the same as they are in a traditional DTS 5.1-channel system.

Surround left

Surround right

Rear

DTS ES

3 When the DTS ES signal data stream is decoded, each of the individual channels (front left, front center, front right, left surround, right surround, and rear) are fed to the appropriate amplifiers. The LFE channel is passed through the receiver to a powered subwoofer.

ENCODER

2 DTS ES differs from Dolby Digital EX in that the single rear channel is discrete, not matrixed. This channel is created and managed as a totally distinct channel and fed into the digital data stream.

Rear channel is discreet.

<200MHz LFE

Front, Surround, and Rear
Many newer movies have 6.1- or 7.1-channel soundtracks, using either the Dolby Digital EX or DTS ES surround sound system. The extra channels are true rear channels, located past the normal surround channels, directly behind the listener. In a 6.1-channel system, a single rear channel is used; in a 7.1-channel system, left and right rear channels are employed. This combination of front, surround (side), and rear channels totally surrounds the listener in a full 360° sound field.

4 Throughout the entire DTS ES process, the rear channel is kept discrete and not mixed in with the other channels. This results in full-frequency sound and accurate separation for that channel; the rear speaker is positioned directly behind the listener.

DECODER

How Dolby Pro Logic Works

1 Before there was Dolby Digital, home theater surround sound was implemented using Dolby Pro Logic technology, a four-channel system, with discrete left and right channels combined with matrixed center and surround channels. Matrix technology uses a *4-2-4 processing system*—the 4 original channels are blended into 2 channels for more efficient distribution and then are decoded for 4 channels of playback. (There is no LFE channel in Dolby Pro Logic.)

Left   Center   Right

Surround

2 The original recording is engineered with four audio channels— left, center, right, and a single surround channel.

3 The audio channels are assigned to four separate data streams: A (left channel), B (right channel), C (center channel), and D (surround channel).

4 The Dolby processor mixes data stream C equally into streams A and B, but 3dB softer than the original. (This is so the center channel information will not overwhelm the left and right channels when played through a traditional two-channel audio system with no surround sound processing.)

ENCODER

6 The two stereo channels (with data streams C and D matrixed into the streams) are encoded onto a DVD, videotape, or television broadcast.

5 The Dolby processor then mixes data stream D equally into streams A and B. Each half of the signal gets a 90° phase shift, with the result that the D data mixed into stream A is 180° out of phase with the D data mixed into stream B. Data stream D also receives a 3dB level reduction and is "band-limited" at 7KHz. (This cuts off the surround channel's treble response, resulting in audio that is less than full-frequency.)

DVD SRC1
DSCRT 6.1 + THX

AV receiver

Matrixed A and B channels

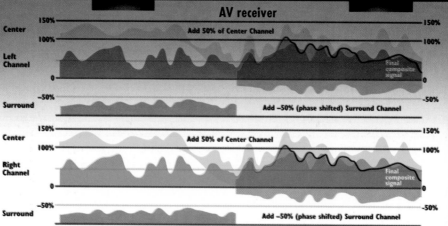

Mixing multiple channels into a single channel

Center

Left Channel

Add 50% of Center Channel

Final composite signal

Surround

Add −50% (phase shifted) Surround Channel

Center

Right Channel

Add 50% of Center Channel

Final composite signal

Surround

Add −50% (phase shifted) Surround Channel

Matrix Versus Discrete

The major drawback to matrix technology is that it's not terribly precise. That's because when everything gets all mixed together, it doesn't always separate out completely, resulting in some degree of leakage from one channel to another. Imagine mixing streams of red, green, blue, and purple sand together in a bucket, carrying the bucket across a room, and then trying to extract the individual colors at the other end—messy at best, and perhaps even impossible to separate into the original colors.

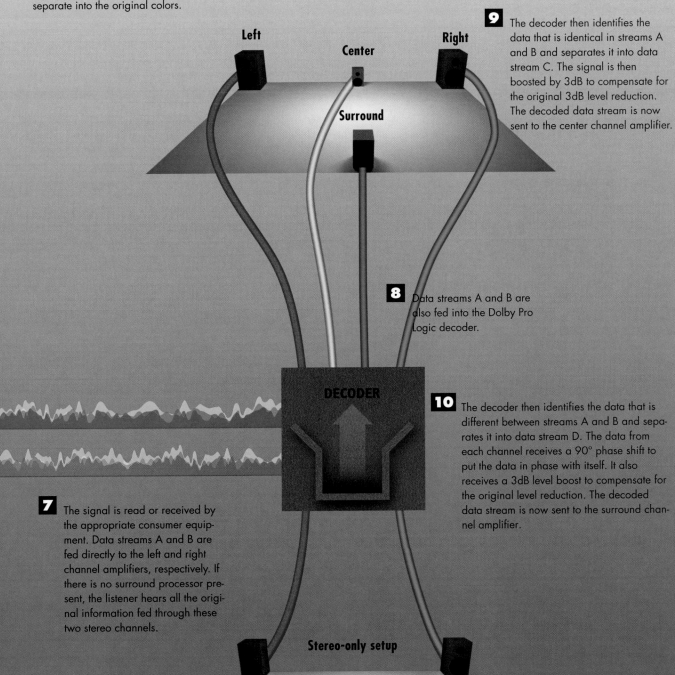

9 The decoder then identifies the data that is identical in streams A and B and separates it into data stream C. The signal is then boosted by 3dB to compensate for the original 3dB level reduction. The decoded data stream is now sent to the center channel amplifier.

Left

Center

Right

Surround

8 Data streams A and B are also fed into the Dolby Pro Logic decoder.

DECODER

10 The decoder then identifies the data that is different between streams A and B and separates it into data stream D. The data from each channel receives a 90° phase shift to put the data in phase with itself. It also receives a 3dB level boost to compensate for the original level reduction. The decoded data stream is now sent to the surround channel amplifier.

7 The signal is read or received by the appropriate consumer equipment. Data streams A and B are fed directly to the left and right channel amplifiers, respectively. If there is no surround processor present, the listener hears all the original information fed through these two stereo channels.

Stereo-only setup

How Dolby Pro Logic IIx Works

1 Dolby Pro Logic IIx expands on the older Dolby Pro Logic system to convert any two-channel music or movie soundtrack into six channels of full-bandwidth surround sound (with two surround channels and a single rear channel). It works by detecting direction cues that occur naturally in stereo content and then uses those cues to simulate five-channel surround playback. It's ideally suited for listening to stereo CDs, non-surround video games, and older (non-Dolby Digital) stereo movies in a home theater environment. The process starts when the programming's original left and right stereo signals are fed into the Dolby Pro Logic IIx processor.

Left   **Right**

DTS Neo:6

DTS distributes a similar pseudo-surround system called DTS Neo:6. By most accounts, DTS Neo:6 is not as effective as Dolby Pro Logic IIx at simulating surround effects.

2 The stereo signal is analyzed for information that is identical between the two channels. This identical information is separated into a new center audio channel.

Processor Servo Circuit

3 A special servo detector circuit in the surround sound processor analyzes steering cues in the front channels to identify sounds that are then sent to the appropriate surround or rear channels. The detector circuit uses multiple steering bands that are steered independently, so that different frequencies can be steered to different channels; higher frequencies (such as gun shots) are steered faster than lower frequencies (such as explosions).

DVD SRC1
DSCRT 6.1 + THX

Dolby Pro Logic IIx receiver

Depth positioning cues are calculated from the stereo input audio streams

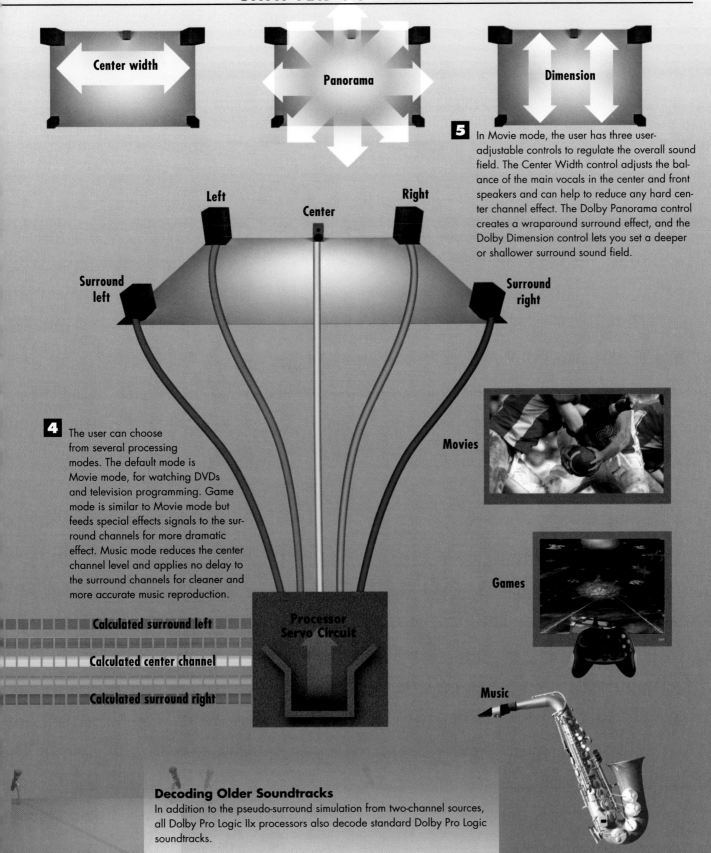

Center width

Panorama

Dimension

5 In Movie mode, the user has three user-adjustable controls to regulate the overall sound field. The Center Width control adjusts the balance of the main vocals in the center and front speakers and can help to reduce any hard center channel effect. The Dolby Panorama control creates a wraparound surround effect, and the Dolby Dimension control lets you set a deeper or shallower surround sound field.

Left

Center

Right

Surround left

Surround right

4 The user can choose from several processing modes. The default mode is Movie mode, for watching DVDs and television programming. Game mode is similar to Movie mode but feeds special effects signals to the surround channels for more dramatic effect. Music mode reduces the center channel level and applies no delay to the surround channels for cleaner and more accurate music reproduction.

Movies

Games

Music

Calculated surround left

Calculated center channel

Calculated surround right

Processor Servo Circuit

Decoding Older Soundtracks
In addition to the pseudo-surround simulation from two-channel sources, all Dolby Pro Logic IIx processors also decode standard Dolby Pro Logic soundtracks.

How Different Surround Sound Formats Compare

DVDs

CDs Games

DVD Movies
- Dolby Digital
- Dolby Digital EX
- DTS ES

Music and Video Games
- Dolby Pro Logic IIx
- DTS Neo:6

HDTV
- Dolby Digital

Broadcast Television
- Dolby Pro Logic
- Dolby Pro Logic IIx
- DTS Neo:6

Surround Format	Number of Channels	Surround Technology	Channels	Typical Uses
Dolby Pro Logic	4	Matrix	Left (discrete, full-bandwidth)	Dolby Surround VHS videotapes
			Right (discrete, full-bandwidth)	Dolby Surround television broadcasts
			Center (matrix, full-bandwidth)	Older Dolby Surround DVDs
			Surround (matrix, limited-bandwidth)	
DTS Neo:6	5.1	Matrix/pseudo-surround	Left (discrete, full-bandwidth)	Stereo VHS videotapes
			Right (discrete, full-bandwidth)	Stereo television broadcasts
			Center (matrix, full-bandwidth)	Older stereo DVDs
			Left surround (matrix, full-bandwidth)	Stereo music CDs
			Right surround (matrix, full-bandwidth)	Video games
			Subwoofer (via bass management technology)	
Dolby Pro Logic IIx	6.1	Matrix/pseudo-surround	Left (discrete, full-bandwidth)	Stereo VHS videotapes
			Right (discrete, full-bandwidth)	Stereo television broadcasts
			Center (matrix, full-bandwidth)	Older stereo DVDs
			Left surround (matrix, full-bandwidth)	Stereo music CDs
			Right surround (matrix, full-bandwidth)	Video games
			Rear (matrix, full-bandwidth)	
			Subwoofer (via bass management technology)	
Dolby Digital	Up to 5.1	Discrete	Left (discrete, full-bandwidth)	Most DVDs
			Right (discrete, full-bandwidth)	Some digital satellite broadcasts
			Center (discrete, full-bandwidth)	All HDTV broadcasts
			Left surround (discrete, full-bandwidth)	
			Right surround (discrete, full-bandwidth)	
			LFE (discrete)	
DTS	5.1	Discrete	Left (discrete, full-bandwidth)	Some DVDs
			Right (discrete, full-bandwidth)	
			Center (discrete, full-bandwidth)	
			Left surround (discrete, full-bandwidth)	
			Right surround (discrete, full-bandwidth)	
			LFE (discrete)	
Dolby Digital EX	6.1 or 7.1	Discrete with matrix rear	Left (discrete, full-bandwidth)	Some DVDs
			Right (discrete, full-bandwidth)	
			Center (discrete, full-bandwidth)	
			Left surround (discrete, full-bandwidth)	
			Right surround (discrete, full-bandwidth)	
			Left rear (matrix, full bandwidth)	
			Right rear (matrix, full bandwidth)	
			LFE (discrete)	
DTS ES	6.1	Discrete	Left (discrete, full-bandwidth)	Some DVDs
			Right (discrete, full-bandwidth)	
			Center (discrete, full-bandwidth)	
			Left surround (discrete, full-bandwidth)	
			Right surround (discrete, full-bandwidth)	
			Rear (discrete, full bandwidth)	
			LFE (discrete)	

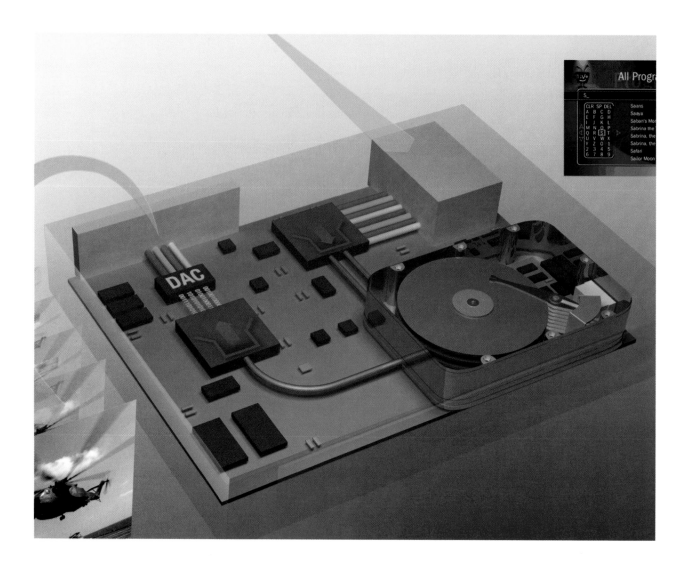

5

HOW AUDIO/VIDEO SOURCES WORK

THE picture on your new home theater system is only as good as the source material you feed to it. That source material can come from an over-the-air antenna (for broadcast television), a cable television signal, a direct broadcast satellite, or a variety of audio and video equipment. In fact, one of the nice things about a state-of-the-art home theater system is the variety of input devices you can use—each of which is typically used for different types of material.

Up until a few years ago, the primary video input device was a videocassette recorder (VCR). Most homes still have a VHS videocassette deck (Beta-format decks being long-since expunged from the market) and a healthy collection of videocassettes, either recorded at home or of the prerecorded variety. The problem with VCRs, however, and the reason they're no longer widely used, is that the picture quality isn't up to snuff—especially when compared to higher-quality sources (such as DVDs) and video displays. This is particularly apparent when playing a VCR on a new HDTV display; even the most tolerant viewer is apt to cringe at the soft, low-resolution VCR picture when compared to just about any other video source.

That doesn't mean that video recorders don't still have a place in your system. Particularly popular are the new breed of digital camcorders that let you record your own home movies and then edit them on your PC. The MiniDV format is far superior to the old VHS cassettes, recording digital picture and sound at least as good as what you find on commercial DVDs. Some high-end camcorders are even capable of recording in the high-definition video (HDV) format, which is as good as anything you'll find on HDTV broadcasts.

Also popular, for quite different reasons, are digital video recorders (DVRs), also known as hard disk recorders (HDRs) or personal video recorders (PVRs). Regardless of which appellation you adopt, this is a device that functions like a mini-computer, complete with its own hard disk. Television programming is recorded onto the hard disk in digital format for crystal-clear playback. You can even use a hard disk recorder to pause "live" programming, essentially by feeding a live signal to the hard disk and then playing it back immediately from the hard disk, rather than watching the live signal directly. Hard disk recorders make recording easy (at least, a lot easier than with a VCR timer) by providing an electronic program guide (EPG) that displays upcoming programs in an easy-to-navigate grid. Just point to the show you want to record and click a button on the remote control; there aren't any cumbersome timers to set!

For most viewers, the most popular video input device today is the DVD player. DVDs are like CDs in that they hold programming information digitally on a small disc that is read by lasers. DVDs are cheap, easy to use, and widely available; most come with a variety of extras (such as audio commentaries, movie trailers, and "making of" documentaries) to enhance the viewing experience. The picture quality is also very good, completely digital, and often enhanced for 16:9 aspect ratio TVs. It isn't quite HDTV quality (not yet, anyway), but it's as good as any standard definition source you can feed your system.

If you want high-definition programming via DVD, two next-generation disc formats are vying for your attention. The Blu-ray Disc and HD DVD formats both offer increased data storage to handle the heavy requirements of high-definition movies. You'll need a new DVD player (or two) to play these formats, but the promise of 1080p movies on your home television is a big draw.

Of course, Blu-ray and HD DVD are competing and noncompatible formats, which means a big format war is at hand. Blu-ray promises up to 50GB of storage on a dual-layer disc and is backed by Sony, Philips, Apple, Pioneer, Samsung, Thomson, Twentieth Century Fox, and the Walt Disney Company. HD DVD promises up to 30GB of storage on a dual-layer disc and is backed by Toshiba, Sanyo, Paramount, Universal, and Warner. Both formats use 4.75" discs—the same diameter as the current DVD format.

Whichever format wins the high-definition DVD war, consumers will be getting much more capacity than is available on today's DVDs: 30/50GB versus the current 8.5GB. That extra capacity is necessary to carry the high-definition picture and digital surround sound of HDTV programming. In fact, both Blu-ray and HD DVD can handle 1080p programming, which is higher quality that today's 1080i HDTV broadcasts. For this reason, forward-thinking consumers will soon be adding high-definition DVD players to their home theater systems.

Finally, many consumers are adding personal computers to their home theater systems, in the form of digital media hubs or Media Center PCs. A home theater PC can take the place of multiple single-use devices, including CD players, DVD players, and hard disk recorders. Music and videos are stored on the device's hard disk and then played back on command. Some media hubs even let you watch TV through the device and record television programming on the device's hard disk. It's a great audio and video source for any home theater system.

CHAPTER

15

How Videotape Recorders Work

VIDEOCASSETTE recorders (VCRs) used to be a staple in just about every American household—and are still common in many living rooms. While VCRs were originally marketed as a way to record television broadcasts, their most common use was for watching prerecorded videocassette movies. (That's how Blockbuster was born!)

In comparison to all the other components of your home theater system, however, the 1/2" VHS-format VCR is very old technology—more than 25 years old, to be precise. The format doesn't offer digital sound or picture, the picture resolution is below even standard broadcast television, and it doesn't offer much in the way of added features or high-tech bells and whistles—which is why the format is now in its declining years.

Let's take a quick look at VHS picture and sound quality. On tapes recorded at the fastest speed (SP, which delivers the best possible quality), horizontal resolution is only 240 lines. Compare this to the 330-line resolution of normal broadcast or cable television, or the 500-line resolution of DVD, and you can see why a VCR's picture looks dull and noisy next to that from other video sources. (And that's just comparing it to standard definition analog sources; the difference between VHS and HDTV is even more significant.)

The home VCR is in the process of being replaced by DVD players (for watching prerecorded movies) and digital hard disk recorders (for recording television programs), both of which we'll examine later in this book. There is one application, however, where videotape continues to rule, and that's home movie making. Most camcorders sold today use some form of videotape-based recording, typically on ultra-small cassettes (much smaller than VHS tapes) and in a digital format.

A camcorder, of course, is that unique blend of video camera and video recorder that lets you make home movies on videocassettes. Most camcorders today record in the MiniDV format, which lays down digital audio and video signals on a cassette small enough to fit in the palm of your hand. This format delivers up to 500 lines of resolution (twice the resolution of traditional VHS), along with digital stereo sound. Because your movies are recorded digitally, you can transfer them (typically via IEEE 1394 FireWire connection) to your home computer and then edit them using digital movie editing software, such as Adobe Premiere or Final Cut Pro. When you record digitally, edit digitally, and then burn your movies to digital DVDs, you keep a fully digital signal path—which results in extremely high-quality picture and sound.

As good as today's MiniDV camcorders are, they still are limited to standard definition recording. For the ultimate picture and sound quality, you can step up to a high-definition camcorder. These high-end (and high-priced) models record in the HDV format, which uses standard MiniDV cassettes but produces either 720p or 1080i resolution, depending on the camcorder. These HDV camcorders also record Dolby Digital surround sound and shoot in the 16:9 aspect ratio. The result? Truly impressive high-definition movies that look every bit as good as professional HDTV programming.

How a VHS VCR Works

1 When the videocassette is inserted into the VCR, a lever on the VCR releases and opens the door on the cassette, exposing the videotape.

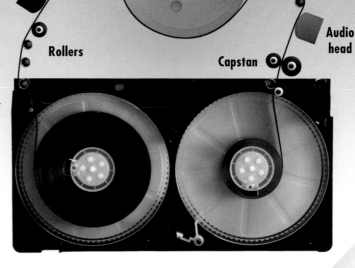

Rotating head drum

Rollers

Erase head

Audio head

Rollers

Capstan

2 The videotape is extracted from the cassette, looped through a series of guides and rollers, and positioned against the VCR's rotating head drum. The tape is pulled past the drum at a speed of 1.31" per second in SP mode, or 0.44" per second in the lower-quality EP mode.

3 The VCR's drum contains two playback heads and two recording heads, positioned 180° apart. The drum rotates at 1,800 RPM (30 revolutions per second) and is tilted in respect to the tape.

Rotating head drum

Helical Scanning

The process of recording data diagonally on the tape using rotating heads is called *helical scanning*. Because of the combination of head rotation and tape movement, the effective speed of the head against the tape is 228.5 inches per second—or about 25 miles per hour! This approach uses much less tape than would a linear scanning approach.

6 For playback, the rotating heads read each successive field of audio and video information and then convert those electrical signals into the audio and video signals that are then sent to your television set for playback.

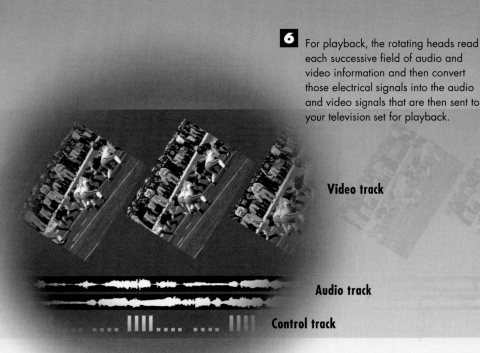

Video track

Audio track

Control track

4 This results in the video and audio signals being recorded on the tape at a diagonal. Each pass of the VCR's rotating head reads the data for one field (one half-frame, or 262.5 scan lines) of the video image. A complete revolution of the two playback heads reads a complete frame of information.

5 Recorded on the tape along with the video signal is the program's audio and control tracks. The control track tells the VCR at which speed the tape was recorded, how quickly to pull the tape past the drum, and how to align the heads during playback. (When you adjust the tracking control of your VCR, you're actually adjusting the skew between this control track and the actual head position against the tape.)

Video track   Audio track   Control track

How a Digital Video Camcorder Works

1 In the camera part of the camcorder, the image is seen through the camera's lens. The higher quality the lens, the more light that is passed through it, without distortion of the image.

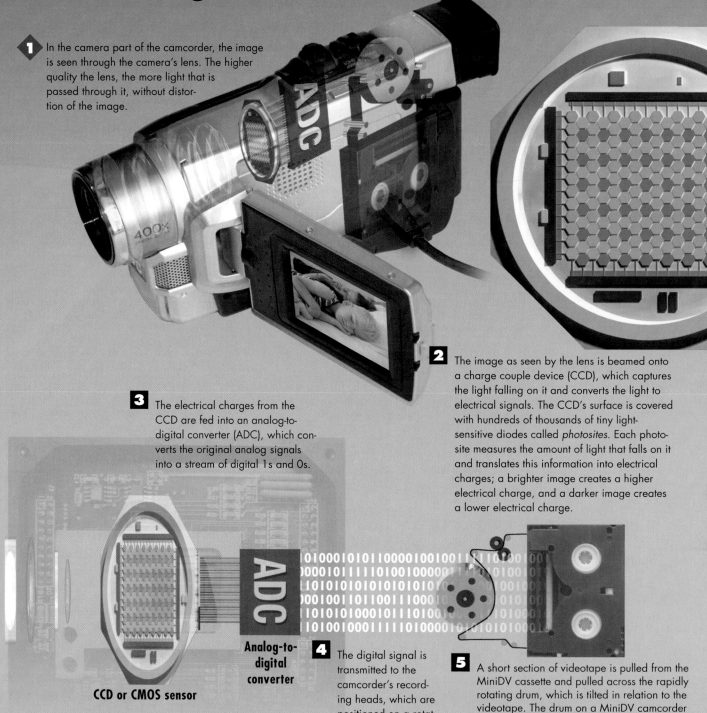

2 The image as seen by the lens is beamed onto a charge couple device (CCD), which captures the light falling on it and converts the light to electrical signals. The CCD's surface is covered with hundreds of thousands of tiny light-sensitive diodes called *photosites*. Each photosite measures the amount of light that falls on it and translates this information into electrical charges; a brighter image creates a higher electrical charge, and a darker image creates a lower electrical charge.

3 The electrical charges from the CCD are fed into an analog-to-digital converter (ADC), which converts the original analog signals into a stream of digital 1s and 0s.

ADC
Analog-to-digital converter

CCD or CMOS sensor

4 The digital signal is transmitted to the camcorder's recording heads, which are positioned on a rotating drum.

5 A short section of videotape is pulled from the MiniDV cassette and pulled across the rapidly rotating drum, which is tilted in relation to the videotape. The drum on a MiniDV camcorder rotates at 9,000 RPM; the tape moves at approximately 0.74 inches per second.

8 The digital audio and video signals can be transferred from the camcorder to a personal computer (typically via an IEEE-1394 FireWire connection), where they can then be edited and manipulated. The edited digital movie can then be burned to DVD for further distribution.

7 Most camcorders today use a digital recording format called MiniDV, which is twice as sharp as the older analog VHS format. A MiniDV cassette can hold up to an hour of audio and video—a total of 11GB of data. Each MiniDV cassette also contains a small memory chip, called *memory in cassette (MIC)*, that is used to record a list of contents, times and dates of recordings, and sample stills from preset edit points.

6 The 1s and 0s of the digital signal are laid down diagonally on the magnetic recording tape; 10 tracks are necessary to record one full frame of NTSC audio and video.

Multiple CCDs
Most consumer-level camcorders use a single CCD to capture the video image. Some high-end camcorders, however, use three CCDs, one for each of the primary colors (red, green, and blue), which provides better detail and color. All professional video cameras use a three-CCD design.

Consumer DV cams

Professional DV cams

CHAPTER

16

How CD and DVD Players Work

A little over 20 years ago, digital technology entered the living rooms of the world. This technology—using computer-like bits and bytes to carry programming information—came on a silvery 5'' disc, and was read by a low-powered laser beam. Chances are, you probably have one of these digital devices somewhere in your home, along with several dozen (or several hundred) of the silvery discs. You call them compact discs, or CDs, and you use them to listen to digitally recorded music.

The CD was a great idea, and the digital technology behind the CD was later adapted to hold more bits per disc, in order to better accommodate video programming. The resulting DVD format has now become the standard for all prerecorded movies.

The picture quality of a DVD is the best you can feed into your home theater system, short of moving to HDTV. DVDs are capable of 500 lines of resolution, which is much better than VHS (240 lines) or broadcast television (330 lines). DVD's picture quality is twice as sharp as a VCR, 50% sharper than what comes over analog cable, and 25% better than what you get off of satellite or digital cable. Plus you get digital surround sound and, in many cases, a widescreen aspect ratio—all for less than twenty bucks a disc!

While the first DVD players cost close to a thousand dollars, today DVD players can be had for well under $100. This drop in price opened the door for affordable DVD players that do more than just single-disc playback—such as the latest trend, the DVD recorder. A DVD recorder lets you not only watch prerecorded DVD movies, but also record your own DVDs. Some DVD recorders include a hard disk recorder, so you can record television programming to the hard disk and then burn those programs to DVD. You can also use a DVD recorder to create DVDs from the home movies you make with a MiniDV camcorder; it's all digital recording, from start to finish.

Know, however, that as great as the existing DVD format is, the picture is strictly standard definition (480i). The current generation of DVDs can store only 8.5GB of data, which isn't nearly enough to reproduce a full high-definition movie. That will soon be rectified, however, by the adoption of a new high-definition DVD format, which will of course obsolete your entire DVD collection!

Currently, two competing high-definition formats are getting set for battle. The Blu-ray Disc format offers 50GB of storage on a dual-layer disc, while the competing HD DVD format offers 30GB of storage—both large enough to store 1080p high-definition programming with multiple tracks of lossless digital audio. Both formats use 4.75'' diameter discs, the same as today's DVD format, and are likely to be backward compatible with current DVD players.

Blu-ray was developed by Sony and is supported by Columbia Tri-Star, MGM, and Disney; HD DVD was developed by Toshiba and NEC and is supported by Time Warner, Universal, and Paramount. There's no predicting which new format will win the war, but expect high-definition DVDs of some sort in your living room by the end of the decade!

How CDs and DVDs Work

1 For both music and movie programming, the original audio or video information is converted into a stream of digital 1s and 0s, using an analog-to-digital converter (ADC). These 1s and 0s are represented as individual pits on the CD or DVD. Both CDs and DVDs are made up of multiple layers sandwiched together into a 5" diameter disc about 1.2 millimeters thick.

CD-ROM

830-nanometer minimum feature size

2 The top layer of the CD is made from a protective acrylic. This nonreadable layer can be printed on, to display the disc's label.

3 The middle layer of the CD is made from reflective aluminum, which covers the pits of the bottom layer. It is this layer that reflects the laser beam projected from the CD player.

4 The bottom layer of a CD is made from an injection-molded piece of clear polycarbonate plastic. The inside surface of this layer is impressed with microscopic pits arranged in a continuous spiral. These pits correspond to the 1s and 0s of the digital signal, and are just 830 nanometers long. Each track is separated from the next by a distance of 1,600 nanometers.

side view of discs

Different Densities

Most commercial DVDs utilize this double-layer, single-sided design. DVDs can also be single-layer, single-sided (without the second, transparent layer); single-layer, double-sided (essentially two single-layer, single-sided discs glued back to back); and double-layer, double-sided (two double-layer, single-sided discs glued back-to-back).

9 The pits on a CD are arranged in a track that forms a single continuous spiral. The pits on a DVD create two separate spiral tracks, one for each layer of the disc. The combination of dual layers and smaller pits mean that much more information can be stored on a DVD than on a CD; the typical CD can store 700MB of data, where a dual-layer, single-sided DVD can store 7.95GB of data—enough space for a four-hour movie!

DVDs can have two spiral tracks on each side.

DVD-ROM

CDs have a single spiral track on one side.

320-nanometer minimum feature size

7 The third layer of the DVD is made from aluminum, which makes it both opaque and reflective. This layer is also impressed with a spiral of microscopic pits, creating a dual-layer disc.

8 The top layer of the DVD, like the top layer of a CD, is made from a protective acrylic. This nonreadable layer can be printed on, to display the disc's label.

5 The bottom layer of a DVD is also made from clear polycarbonate plastic that provides a foundation for the other layers.

6 The second layer of the DVD is made from transparent film, which enables the DVD player's laser to both read the layer and focus through the layer to the next layer. Impressed onto this film is a series of microscopic pits arranged in a continuous spiral, moving out from the center of the disc. The pits on a DVD are much smaller and more tightly compressed than those on a CD; each pit is just 320 nanometers wide and no more than 400 nanometers long. Only 740 nanometers separate one track from another.

How High-Definition DVDs Work

The future of DVD entertainment is high-definition. To deliver high-definition programming on DVDs, we can turn to either of two competing formats—Blu-ray Disc or HD DVD.

1 High-definition programming requires more data storage space than a standard definition movie does. A standard 135-minute movie in high-definition requires 13GB of storage, while lossless digital audio tracks require up to 5GB. Additional storage is required for audio commentary tracks, foreign language tracks, and various disc extras.

2 Current dual-layer DVDs can hold only 8.5GB of data. The HD DVD format holds 30GB on a dual-layer disc, whereas the Blu-ray format holds a whopping 50GB on a dual-layer disc.

CD	DVD	HD-DVD	Blu-ray
0.7GB	8.5GB	30GB	50GB

CD

1.6μm track pitch

Polycarbonate layer

DVD

Data layer 2

Data layer 1

Polycarbonate layer

0.74μm track pitch

HD-DVD

Data layer 2

Data layer 1

Polycarbonate layer

0.45μm track pitch

CD

1.2mm thick

Data layer
Polycarbonate layer

DVD

Polycarbonate layer
Data layer
Data layer
Polycarbonate layer

Data layers

HD-DVD

Top of

Polycarbonate layer
Data layer
Data layer
Polycarbonate layer

Bottom of

side view of discs

3 An HD DVD is the same thickness as a standard DVD, with similar construction. The data layer is sandwiched between two polycarbonate layers, but the pits are about half the size as those on a standard DVD—just 0.15 microns long.

5 During playback, both Blu-ray and HD DVD discs use blue lasers, which have a shorter wavelength than the red lasers used in traditional DVD players. The smaller blue beam can focus more precisely than the older red beam, enabling it to read information in either format's smaller pits.

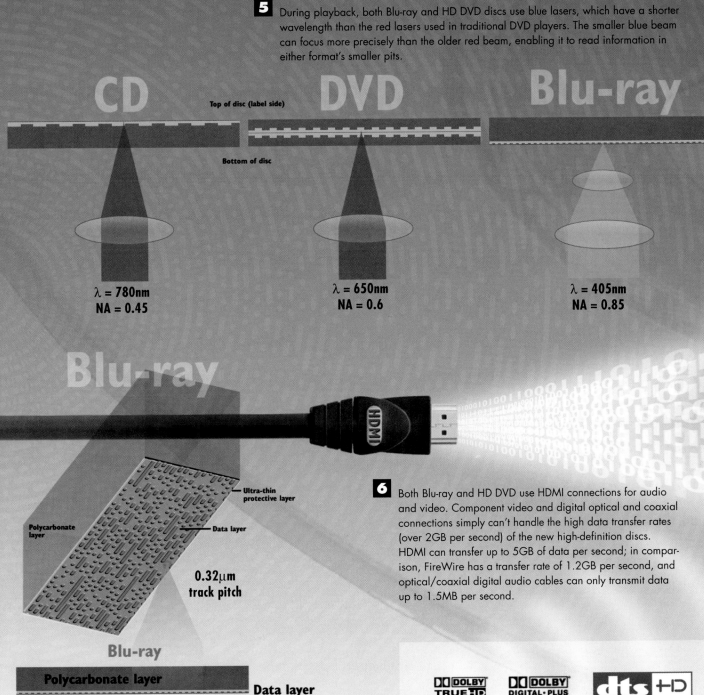

CD

DVD

Blu-ray

Top of disc (label side)

Bottom of disc

$\lambda = 780nm$
$NA = 0.45$

$\lambda = 650nm$
$NA = 0.6$

$\lambda = 405nm$
$NA = 0.85$

Blu-ray

Ultra-thin protective layer

Polycarbonate layer

Data layer

$0.32\mu m$ track pitch

Blu-ray

Polycarbonate layer

Data layer

6 Both Blu-ray and HD DVD use HDMI connections for audio and video. Component video and digital optical and coaxial connections simply can't handle the high data transfer rates (over 2GB per second) of the new high-definition discs. HDMI can transfer up to 5GB of data per second; in comparison, FireWire has a transfer rate of 1.2GB per second, and optical/coaxial digital audio cables can only transmit data up to 1.5MB per second.

4 A Blu-ray disc is also the same 1.2mm thickness as a standard DVD or HD DVD disc, but the construction is much different. A Blu-ray disc places the data layer on the bottom of the disc, with a thick, protective polycarbonate layer on top. This puts the data closer to the laser beam during playback, which enables more pits to be encoded on the data layer.

HD Sound

In addition to high-definition video (up to 1080p resolution), both Blu-ray and HD DVD discs deliver higher-quality digital audio via the new Dolby Digital Plus, Dolby TrueHD, and DTS HD high-bit rate surround sound formats.

How a DVD Player Works

1 The DVD is rotated rapidly by the DVD player's drive motor. The rotation speed varies between 200 and 500 RPM, depending on which track of the disc is being read.

Laser assembly follows spiral track.

Drive spindle

DVD

4 Where the laser beam hits a pit on the disc, the indentation scatters the light in all directions; no information is read.

2 A laser diode generates a concentrated beam of light through a lens and a focusing coil. This red laser beam has a shorter wavelength than the laser in a CD player, which makes the beam narrow enough to read the smaller pits on a DVD disc.

3 The laser beam is first focused on the disc's transparent layer, through the transparent bottom layer of the disc.

5 Where the laser beam hits a flat area on the disc, it is reflected back to a light sensing diode. This diode converts the pulses of light energy into bursts of electricity, in a digital series of 1s (on) and 0s (off).

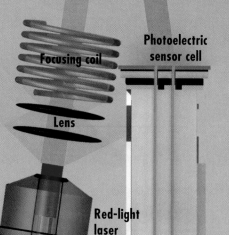

Focusing coil

Photoelectric sensor cell

Lens

Red-light laser

Synchronized Spinning
The DVD player's motor constantly varies the rate at which the DVD spins, so that the disc is always moving at the same speed relative to the laser and detector assembly, regardless of whether the assembly is located under the outside or the inside of the disc.

200rpm on
inner tracks

Up to 500rpm
on outer tracks

7 The electrical signals generated from the reading of the disc are fed through a digital-to-analog converter (DAC), which changes the digital stream into analog audio and video signals. The analog signals are then sent to the other audio and video components of the home theater system. (DVD players with HDMI or DVI connections skip the DAC to output a pure digital data stream to the television or A/V receiver.)

6 After the transparent layer is completely read, the current flowing to a magnetic coil around the laser is changed. This refocuses the beam on the reflective layer of the disc. The beam now reads all the pits on this second layer.

DAC

How a DVD Recorder Works

Close-up of a single-layer recordable DVD disc

Dye layer

Label layer

Reflective layer

Only areas where the dye has been bleached will allow the laser light through

Unbleached areas diffuse laser light

Bleached area

1 A blank DVD has a single recordable layer made from a dyed color material. (This dye layer is why blank DVDs are often purple in color.) On top of this dyed layer is a thin layer of gold, which functions to reflect the laser beam. These layers are surrounded by protective top and bottom plastic layers.

Polycarbonate protective layer

2 The DVD recorder generates a red laser beam with a wavelength of 635–650 nanometers, which it aims at the recordable dye layer of the disc, following a spiral groove outward from the center of the disc.

3 The laser beam doesn't create pits on the disc, but rather bleaches the dye where it hits the disc. This changes the transparency of the spot to form a distortion, called a *stripe*, along the spiral track.

4 These distorted areas in the dye layer correspond to the pits on a commercial DVD; they reflect less light than the unchanged areas surrounding them. When the DVD player's laser beam reads the newly recorded disc, the beam is scattered by the stripes; only the unchanged areas of the disc are read, just like in a commercial DVD.

Single-layer recordable DVD disc

Dual-layer recordable DVD disc

5 Most current DVD recorders can only write to single-layer discs; this limits the disc's capacity to just 4.7GB, or only about an hour of video. Some newer DVD recorders, however, use a more powerful laser that can write dual-layer discs with close to 8GB capacity, long enough to hold a two-hour movie.

Label layer

Reflective layer

Bleached area

Dye layer 2

Close-up of a dual-layer recordable DVD disc

Dye layer 1

Polycarbonate protective layer

Only areas where the dye has been bleached will allow the laser light through

Unbleached areas diffuse laser light

Rewriteable Discs

Rewritable discs are different from recordable discs in that you can re-record over previously recorded discs. Instead of a dye layer, rewriteable discs use a layer of crystalline material. The laser beam essentially melts selected areas of the crystal, turning these into non-crystalline areas that function similarly to the pits in a commercial DVD. To rewrite a disc, a lower-energy laser beam is used to loosen the changed material so that it recrystallizes to its original state.

CHAPTER
17

How Digital Video Recorders Work

A digital video recorder, or DVR, is like a VCR without the tape. Instead, programming is recorded on a hard disk, like the kind used in personal computers. The hard disk records programs digitally, which means that the recording can be identical to the original, with no loss in audio or video quality.

Hard disk recording offers several other advantages to recording on tape. One big benefit is instant access to any point in the recording. With a videocassette, which offers sequential access only, you have to fast forward and rewind the tape to get to the exact point you want; with hard disk recording's random access, moving to any specified point in the recording is instantaneous, just like cueing up a new song on a CD. The hard disk also enables crystal-clear special effects, such as freeze frame, slow motion, fast forward, and rewind—all with the same picture quality as the original program.

DVRs also let you pause and rewind "live" programming. The word *live* is in quotation marks because you can't really pause programming as it arrives over the airwaves or via cable. What you can do, however, is immediately record that live program to the DVR's hard disk, and then watch the playback of the program from the hard disk instead of from your television's tuner. Since the DVR uses separate write and read heads to put information on and read information from the hard disk, the playback of the recorded material only lags a millisecond behind the original broadcast. Then, when you hit the pause button, you're pausing the playback from the hard disk. It's like you're pausing the live broadcast, although you really aren't.

Recording television programming is a lot easier on a DVR than on a VCR, thanks to the DVR's electronic program guide (EPG). The EPG is a listing of upcoming programming across all available channels, up to a week or more in advance. Recording a program is as easy as locating and selecting the program in the EPG. Most EPGs also enable you to search for specific shows and opt to record all broadcasts of your favorite shows with the click of a single button. It's a lot easier than setting the timer on a VCR!

The most popular DVRs use the TiVo EPG. (In fact, TiVo is so popular that the brand name has become a verb, as in "I'm going to TiVo that program tonight.") But TiVo isn't the only type of DVR available today. Many consumer electronics companies manufacture either freestanding DVRs or devices that incorporate both hard disk and DVD recorders. In addition, most cable companies offer set top boxes with built-in hard disk recorders, as do the two major direct broadcast satellite systems. There are even some television manufacturers that are starting to include hard disk recorders in their big-screen television sets! It's a great technology, and very popular with television lovers everywhere.

How Hard Disk Recording Works

1 The broadcast television, cable, or satellite signal feeds into the tuner or video input of the DVR.

Record Two Programs at Once
Many DVRs incorporate two separate tuners, in order to record two programs simultaneously.

Output panel

MPEG encoder

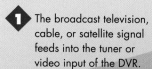

DAC

MPEG decoder

7 This data is then converted back into analog audio and video signals and fed through the DVR's output connections to the television set for viewing.

6 To play back a recording, the read portion of the read/write head accesses the desired data and reads the magnetic particles on the disk.

2 The DVR displays an electronic program guide, which the viewer uses to select which programs to record.

Input tuners

3 At the designated time, the DVR turns itself on and switches to the correct input and channel for recording.

Read/write heads

Actuator arms

Magnetic platters

4 The heart of the DVR is the hard disk, which operates just like a hard disk on a personal computer. Magnetic platters within the hard disk rotate at speeds of up to 7,200 RPM; a head actuator pushes and pulls the multiple read/write heads (attached to read/write arms) across the surface of the spinning platters.

5 The write portion of the read/write head converts the incoming audio/video signals into a series of electrical impulses. These impulses rearrange the magnetic particles on the hard disk into a pattern of digital 1s and 0s corresponding to the original audio and video signals.

How You Can Pause "Live" Television

1 One of the favorite features of a DVR is the ability to pause "live" television. The DVR can't actually affect the live television feed, but it can approximate the effect of pausing a live broadcast by cleverly manipulating the data it records on its hard drive. The process starts by automatically sending the audio and video signal from whatever program you're watching directly to the hard disk.

2 A section of the DVR's hard disk is devoted to a continually changing buffer of automatically recorded programming, reflecting whichever channel is currently selected on the DVR's tuner. This buffer might contain anywhere from a few minutes up to an hour's worth of programming and is created automatically, without the knowledge of the viewer.

3 As soon as the write portion of the read/write head records the current programming, the read section of the head can then read this same data. Thus the newly recorded program is played back from the hard disk, virtually instantaneously with the recording itself; the gap between recording and playback is less than a second.

Read head

Write head

Total Control

Since the viewer is watching a playback of a recorded program, he can use all the access features of the DVR, including rewind and fast forward. (He can only fast forward up to the current point of the recording, of course.) In addition, many DVRs feature a Live button that returns the playback to the current point of recording.

5 Some DVRs offer a commercial skip feature. When the viewer presses the Skip button, the playback automatically skips forward 30 or 60 seconds, thus bypassing any commercials recorded along with the program.

SKIP OVER COMMERCIALS!

4 While the viewer thinks he is watching the live program, he's actually watching the near-instantaneous playback of the recorded program from the hard disk. When the viewer presses the pause button on the remote control, the DVR pauses the playback of the recorded program. This has the effect of pausing the "live" programming, even though it's only the playback that's being paused. The recording of the live program continues, uninterrupted.

Paused frame

How TiVo and Other Electronic Program Guides Work

1 An electronic program guide is simply a schedule of upcoming television programs across all available channels in your area, or on your cable or satellite system. This guide is presented as a grid, usually with channels along the left side and times along the right side. Most EPGs display programming up to at least a week in advance.

Programming guide

Creating the Guide

The programming information for the EPG is provided by a third-party service, such as TiVo or TV Guide Online. This service obtains the programming schedules from the broadcast networks and local stations, and uses the information to compile its proprietary guide.

5 Most EPGs contain more than just the program title and start time. When you click your DVR's Information button, the EPG displays more detailed information about the selected program.

6 Some EPGs let you browse the listings by channel number, channel name, or program title.

2 The EPG can only display a limited number of channels and times on the screen. You display additional channels by scrolling down through the channel list. You display programming further in advance by scrolling right through the hours of the day.

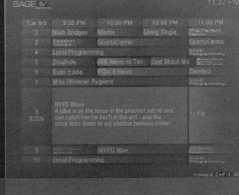

PVR

SDTV

Remote control

4 To record a program, you first have to locate the program on the EPG's schedule. Then you either click the program and select Record from the onscreen menu, or simply select the program and click the Record button on the DVR's remote control.

3 Scheduling information for the EPG is downloaded automatically by your DVR at preselected intervals. For example, your DVR might update the EPG every night at midnight. Depending on the EPG, new information might be downloaded via phone line, from the Internet, or as part of a broadcast signal.

8 Many EPGs let you opt to record the same program every week, all instances of the program on the current channel, all instances of the program on all channels, or only new episodes of the program (no reruns).

7 You can also search for a specific program—even if you don't know what channel it's on!

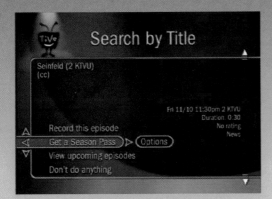

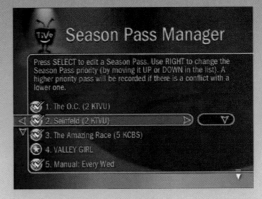

CHAPTER
18

How Digital Media Servers Work

DIGITAL audio is a big deal, especially if you have a portable audio player (like the iPod) or download music from the Internet to your computer. Until recently, the world of digital music had been entirely separate from the world of home audio and home theater systems. Fortunately, we're living in a world of converging technologies—in this instance, the convergence of computer technology and home audio technology. The result is a new family of devices that let you play digital music through your home audio or home theater system.

Playing digital music through your home audio system is a logical extension to playing the same digital audio files on your computer. The difference is that, instead of listening to the music through the tinny speakers attached to your PC, you listen through the big speakers and high-powered amplifier in your home audio system.

Three types of devices let you play digital audio files on your home theater system. The first type of unit is called a *digital media server*. This is a self-contained unit that has a built-in hard disk and CD drive. You insert a CD into the drive, burn it to the built-in hard disk, and then play songs from the hard disk. This type of unit typically looks like a regular consumer audio component and connects to your home audio system via digital or analog connections.

The second type of device is actually a type of personal computer, called a *Media Center PC*. This is a computer optimized for use in your living room. It looks like a normal audio component but works like a computer; it uses a special interface designed for living room use and is operated by a wireless remote control. A Media Center PC can actually replace several standard components because it functions as a CD player and burner, DVD player (and sometimes burner), CD jukebox, television tuner, and DVR—all in a single box!

The final type of device is called a *media hub*, and it doesn't have a built-in hard disk or CD drive. Instead, it connects to your home computer network, accesses the digital audio files stored on your PC's hard disk, and then streams the music through your home audio system. This type of hub is typically a small and relatively low-cost device that connects directly to your home audio system; it plugs in to your home network via either wired or wireless connection.

In addition, many new A/V receivers now let you connect your iPod or other portable audio player directly to the receiver. With this type of setup, you control your iPod with the receiver's remote control and view song and artist information on your TV screen. It's a convenient way to listen to your iPod music without connecting your computer to your home theater system.

Whichever type of device you choose, you'll need to convert your CD collection to digital audio files. This means choosing an audio file format—and there are several to choose from. The most popular formats for portable use (MP3, WMA, and AAC) compress the original music to a degree that's quite noticeable when played on a full-fidelity home audio system. This is why many users choose a format that either exactly retains the original file information (WAV) or incorporates lossless compression (WMA Lossless or FLAC) that retains the original fidelity while reducing the file size by half. You don't want to spend big bucks on a home theater system and then treat yourself to inferior sound!

How Digital Audio Works

Analog input

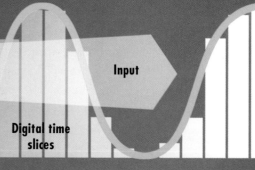

Input

Digital time slices

1 All digital recordings—starting in the recording studio—are made by creating digital samples of the original sound. An analog-to-digital converter (ADC) "listens" to the original analog signal and takes a digital snapshot of the music at a particular point in time. The length of that snapshot (measured in bits) and the number of snapshots per second (called the *sampling rate*) determine the quality of the reproduction. The more samples per second, the more accurate the resulting digital "picture" of the original music.

Output

4 When you copy a digital audio file, you can either copy the file exactly or use some sort of compression to reduce the otherwise-huge file sizes. (A typical 3-minute song recorded at 44.1KHz takes up 32MB.) The best audio fidelity comes from using a non-compressed file format, such as WAV or AIF.

5 Lossy compression works by sampling the original file and removing those ranges of sounds that the average listener can't hear, based on accepted psychoacoustic models. You control the sound quality and the size of the resulting file by selecting different sampling rates for the data. The lower the sampling rate, the smaller the file size—and the lower the sound quality. Popular file formats that use lossy compression include MP3, AAC, and WMA.

Original audio

Largest file size

Uncompressed

Original audio

Smallest file size

Lossy compression

ADC

Binary encoding of time slices

2 All these bits are converted into a data file that is then copied onto some sort of storage medium. In the case of CDs, the storage medium is the compact disc itself; you can also store this digital audio data in computer memory, on a hard disk drive, or on the storage media of a portable audio player.

Digital audio file

Input

DAC

Output

3 On playback, the digital audio file is converted back into analog format by a digital-to-analog converter (DAC). DACs can be found in CD players, A/V receivers, portable audio players, and PC sound cards.

6 If you want to create a high-fidelity digital archive, a better solution is to use a lossless compression format. These formats work similar to Zip compression; redundant bits are taken out to create the compressed file, which is then uncompressed for playback. The resulting file has exact fidelity to the original, while still being stored in a smaller-sized file. Popular lossless file formats include WMA Lossless, ALAC, and FLAC.

Original audio

Medium file size

Lossless compression

Bit Rate

When you multiply the sampling rate by the sample size and the number of channels (two for stereo), you end up with a *bit rate*. For example, compact discs sample music 44,100 times per second, for a 44.1KHz sampling rate; each sample is 16 bits long. Multiply $44,100 \times 16 \times 2$ and you get a bit rate of 1,400,000 bits per second—or 1,400Kbps.

How a Media Server Works

1 A digital media server is a dedicated device that serves as a digital audio jukebox for your home theater system. Most servers let you store music on an internal hard disk or access music stored on other devices in your home.

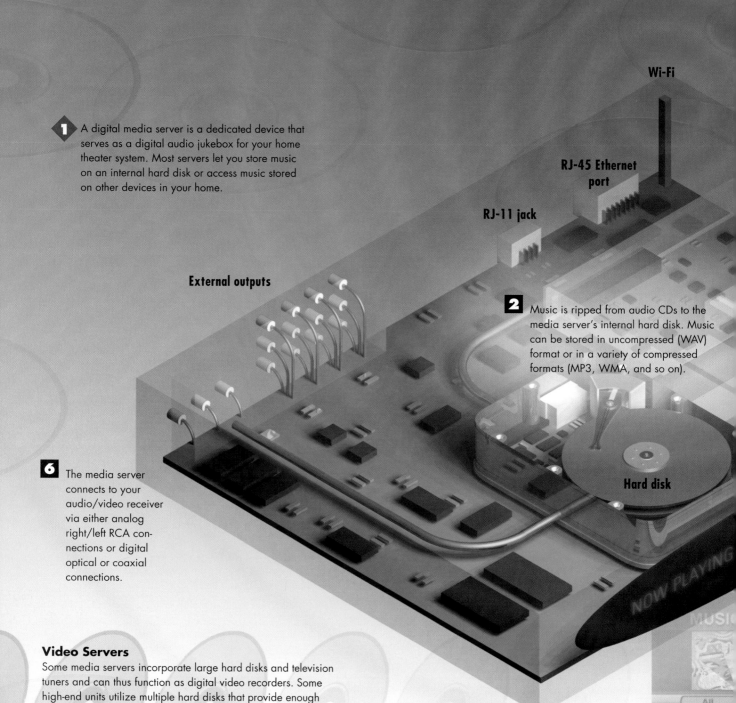

Wi-Fi

RJ-45 Ethernet port

RJ-11 jack

External outputs

2 Music is ripped from audio CDs to the media server's internal hard disk. Music can be stored in uncompressed (WAV) format or in a variety of compressed formats (MP3, WMA, and so on).

Hard disk

6 The media server connects to your audio/video receiver via either analog right/left RCA connections or digital optical or coaxial connections.

NOW PLAYING

MUSIC

All

All My

Bill's

Crazy

Steve

John

Video Servers
Some media servers incorporate large hard disks and television tuners and can thus function as digital video recorders. Some high-end units utilize multiple hard disks that provide enough capacity to store an entire library of DVDs.

3 The media server connects to your home network via either Wi-Fi (wireless) or Ethernet (wired) connection. Once connected to your network, the server can access digital audio files stored on other PCs in your home.

4 The network connection also enables the media server to access the Internet to download information about ripped CDs—including track names, artist info, and album cover art.

CD-ROM drive

CD-ROM

5 Access to any album or song stored on the media server is done via an onscreen display. Most onscreen displays let you sort music by album, artist, or genre; you can also create your own custom playlists of music.

How a Media Center PC Works

7 The Media Center PC connects to your home network and the Internet via Wi-Fi (wireless) or Ethernet (wired) connection. It can access files stored on other PCs in your home or play back audio and video via Media Center Extender units.

Wi-Fi

1 A Media Center PC combines multiple functions into a single device—CD jukebox, DVD player, and DVR. Media Center PCs differ from desktop PCs in that they're quieter, easier to use, and designed to look and feel like living room audio/video components.

2 The Media Center's CD drive lets you play music CDs. Media Center PCs with a CD burner let you create your own custom CDs from songs stored on the PC's hard disk.

3 The combination of CD drive and hard disk lets you rip music CDs to the Media Center PC's hard drive. The resulting digital audio files can then be played back in any order, much like a digital music jukebox.

DVD/CD-ROM drive

4 The Media Center PC's DVD drive lets you play DVD movies, as you would in a standalone DVD player. Typically, Windows Media Player is used to play back DVDs.

5 Most Media Center PCs include one or more television tuners, for either standard definition or high definition broadcasts. Television viewing is made easier with the PC's electronic program guide.

6 The combination of TV tuner and hard disk lets you use the Media Center PC as a digital video recorder. Use the EPG to select programs to record; the programs are then automatically saved to the PC's hard disk, where they can be viewed at your leisure. The Media Center PC has all the functionality of a standalone DVR, including the capability to pause "live" broadcasts.

Network connections

TV tuner

Outputs

CPU

Hard drive

8 Most Media Center PCs are controlled by the Windows XP Media Center Edition operating system. Windows Media Center is designed with a 10-foot interface and is operated by a consumer-friendly remote control. No computer experience is necessary.

It's Also a PC!
Don't forget that a Media Center PC is still a PC. You can minimize the Windows Media Center interface and use regular Windows XP to surf the Internet and perform standard computer operations.

How a Media Hub Works

1 Music files are stored on a personal computer elsewhere in your home, using one of the common digital audio file formats. This PC is connected to your home network.

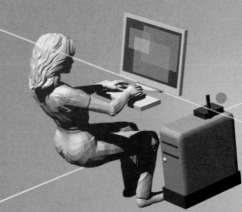

Networked PC

Wi-Fi hub

2 The media hub, which is located next to your other home theater components, also connects to your home network, typically via a wireless Wi-Fi connection.

7 You can connect multiple media hubs in different rooms throughout your house. Each media hub can play a different mix of music, letting you create a whole house audio system via Wi-Fi.

Wi-Fi–enabled media hub

6 The selected digital music is transmitted over the home network to the media hub, where it is sent to the A/V receiver for playback.

5 The media hub uses your home network to connect to the main PC and queue up songs for playback.

4 You use the media hub's remote control (and either an onscreen or a front-panel display) to operate the hub's media player software. You can then select which songs and playlists (stored on the other PC) you want to play on your home theater system.

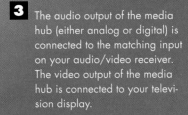

3 The audio output of the media hub (either analog or digital) is connected to the matching input on your audio/video receiver. The video output of the media hub is connected to your television display.

Media Center Extenders
If your main PC is running Windows XP Media Center Edition, you can use a specialized type of media hub called a *Media Center Extender*. This device works just like a normal media hub but uses the Windows Media Center software to control all the operations.

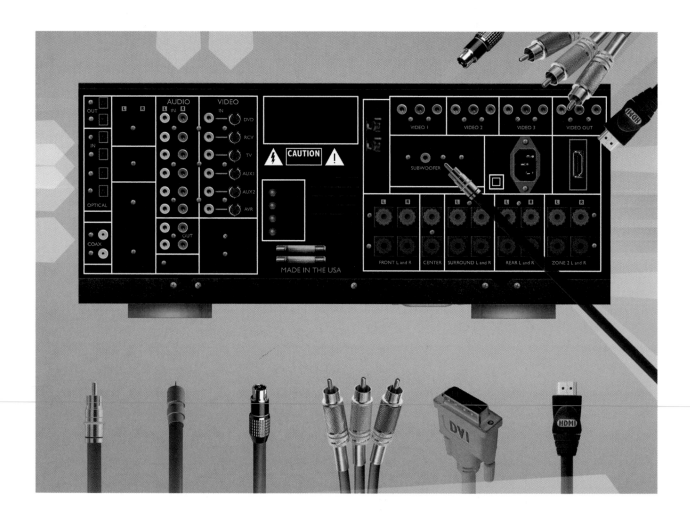

P A R T

HOW HOME THEATER SYSTEMS WORK

HOME theater means different things to different people. To some, hooking up a DVD player to a 26" stereo TV creates a home theater. To others, home theater is a complete system that includes a projection TV and surround-sound audio system. To still others, a home theater system consists of a dedicated room with theater-style seating, a huge front projection screen, and a popcorn machine in the lobby.

The reality is, home theater is whatever you want it to be—as long as it helps achieve one basic goal. That goal is to reproduce in your home, as accurately as possible, the experience of watching a film in a movie theater. How you achieve this goal is at the heart of audio/video system design, and you can spend as much or as little as you want to achieve that goal.

That said, the minimum requirements for an acceptable home theater system today include a fairly large television or video display capable of reproducing HDTV signals with a 16:9 aspect ratio; a multiple-speaker surround sound system, driven by an audio/video receiver; and a variety of high-quality video and audio sources, including (but not limited to) a digital cable or satellite connection, a DVD player, a hard disk digital video recorder, and a source for high-definition television signals.

Naturally, there are lots of different choices for each of the basic parts of your home theater system, as well as many other components you can add to your system to increase your viewing and listening enjoyment. For example, how do you define a "fairly large television"? If you're currently watching a 19" TV, a 26" model would seem fairly large to you. Other folks, however, might say that you really need a 42" or larger 16:9 ratio screen for home theater viewing; still others might spec a 55" screen as the bare minimum. For all parts of your system, what you end up with depends on your personal tastes, your personal budget, and the type of room you're working with.

Which components you choose affects how much your total system will cost, of course. While it's possible to build a bare-bones home theater system for less than $1,000, it's more likely that you'll have to move into the $2,500–$5,000 range to attain acceptable performance—and it's not unheard of for high-end systems to cost $25,000 or more. As with anything else in life, you get what you pay for—and if you want state-of-the-art home theater performance, you'll have to shell out some big bucks.

The type of home theater system you want will influence where you buy it. You can shop for low- and mid-priced systems at one of the big consumer electronics chains or on the Internet, but if you're interested in a higher-end system, you need to look for a specialty audio/video retailer or custom installer. In general, the more sophisticated the equipment you want, the better trained the retailer you'll want to buy from. Don't expect a bargain outlet to know all the ins and outs of building a custom home theater.

At the top of the retail chain is the custom home theater installer. These pros fly in some rarified air and typically handle high-end equipment you just won't find anyplace else. A custom installer will handle your complete system, from concept through installation, in some cases including remodeling your home's interior to best fit your new system. If you're concerned about price, find another place to shop; you'll get superb service here, but you'll pay for it.

Once you purchase all the individual components, you need to connect and configure them appropriately. The basic theory is simple, even if all the ultimate connections aren't. Basically, you feed the output signal from each audio and video source to the input connections on your audio/video receiver. Then you feed the video output from your receiver to the matching input on your television set. Finally, the speaker outputs on your receiver connect to the matching inputs on each of your speakers.

The types of connections you use is another variable in the equation. If you look on the back of a new A/V receiver, you'll see a multiplicity of input and output jacks. For audio connections, you have the traditional right and left RCA jacks, as well as newer optical and coaxial digital connections. There are even more video connection options, ranging from RF (coaxial) and composite video to S-Video and component video. Some newer receivers also offer digital DVI and HDMI video connections. Given the choice, you want to use digital connections whenever possible; also popular are three-cable component connections for high-quality video.

Once everything is connected, you can control it all via remote control. Instead of juggling multiple remotes for each of your components, consider consolidating with a universal or learning remote that can control multiple components. The most advanced remotes offer programmable interfaces and single-button control of complex operations, via multiple-component macros. That's the way to go—press one button for "Movies" and watch your TV, A/V receiver, and DVD player turn on, switch to the appropriate inputs, and start playing!

19

How to Set Up a Home Theater System

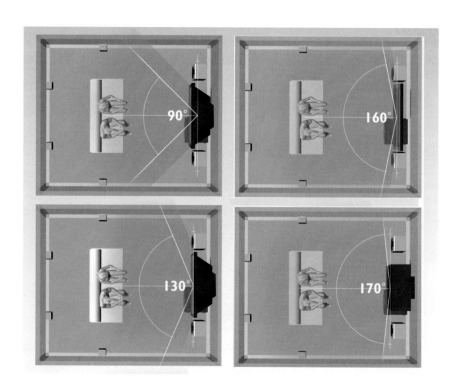

AS you plan your home theater layout, you'll need to position your video display, speakers, and furniture carefully to create the best possible viewing and listening experience. In general, you should center your seating area between the side walls on which you mount your surround speakers. The distance from your viewing screen to the center of your seating area should be roughly twice the diagonal measure of a widescreen TV. So, for example, if you have a 60" diagonal television, you'd want to position your main seating about 120", or 10', from the screen.

It's important to eliminate any items that might come between you and the television screen, and between you and each of the speakers. You should minimize anything that might disrupt the direct transmission of sound waves, as well as remove any objects that interfere with your line of sight to the TV screen.

You'll also want to make sure your antenna, satellite dish, or cable line runs into the area where you'll be positioning your TV and other components. The last thing you want is to string an ugly piece of coax cable from one wall to another; it's best to have your cable or satellite installer run the proper connections to the designated place within your wall (or under your floor, if you have a basement or crawl space) beforehand.

Also critical is the positioning of one or more power outlets directly behind your TV and component rack. Because you probably have more components than you have power outlets, an extension power strip is a good idea—even better is a power strip that includes a built-in surge suppressor. This way, your expensive equipment will be protected in case of a power surge.

You should also make sure there's a phone jack behind your system cabinet. Most folks don't think about this, but several components—in particular, digital satellite receivers and hard disk DVRs—have to dial into their specific services on a daily basis. If you have more than one of these devices, you'll probably have to purchase an adapter that lets you plug two or three phones into a single jack, so you can get all your equipment jacked into the phone line.

If you're planning a new installation, it is also important to run an Ethernet connection to your home theater components. Many components can connect to your home network to share audio and video files (and download information from the Internet), which makes an Ethernet connection essential—unless, that is, your components can connect wirelessly, via Wi-Fi.

Probably the most challenging part of the setup process is connecting all the speakers. The front speakers are usually easy enough, but running wires to surround speakers is never fun or easy. You may need to run speaker wire under the carpet or feed it up through a basement or crawl space or down from the attic. When you get into feeding the wire through the wall and out again, you're into a lot of work—which is probably necessary, but a chore nonetheless.

Finally, if all this positioning and cabling and calibrating makes you nervous, bite the bullet and call a professional installer. They do this sort of thing for a living, have all the proper tools, and know all sorts of shortcuts and workarounds that you'll never stumble across. In addition, a professional installer can help you create a great-looking system, especially if you like the look of built-in components and custom furniture. It'll cost, but the results are worth it!

How to Create the Perfect Home Theater Room

1 Enclosed spaces work best. Rooms without defined walls (that is, rooms that lead seamlessly into other rooms) not only lack surfaces on which to mount speakers, but also "leak" a tremendous amount of sound. In addition, the larger area you try to fill with sound, the more amplifier power you need; it's easier to fill a smaller space than it is a larger one.

2 Try to avoid spaces that are perfectly square or that have one dimension exactly twice another. These types of spaces can produce unwanted resonances that can muddy your system's sound.

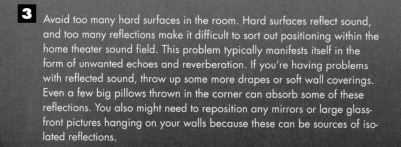

3 Avoid too many hard surfaces in the room. Hard surfaces reflect sound, and too many reflections make it difficult to sort out positioning within the home theater sound field. This problem typically manifests itself in the form of unwanted echoes and reverberation. If you're having problems with reflected sound, throw up some more drapes or soft wall coverings. Even a few big pillows thrown in the corner can absorb some of these reflections. You also might need to reposition any mirrors or large glass-front pictures hanging on your walls because these can be sources of isolated reflections.

4 Be conscious of extraneous noises in the room. You may be used to the noise made by the pump in your fish tank, but it can detract from your enjoyment of watching a quiet movie or listening to a soft CD. Use your ears to isolate and eliminate unnecessary sources of sound.

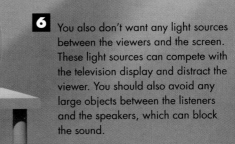

5 Beware of too much light in the room. Direct light sources can reflect off the TV screen—or affect your peripheral vision—and interfere with your viewing. Turn on all the lights in your room and then stare into a blank screen; if you see any lights reflected back at you, turn them off or move them. In addition, closing the drapes and dimming the lights is a good idea before you watch a movie. The darker the room, the more your vision can focus on the activity on the TV screen.

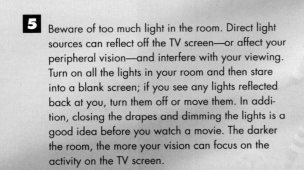

6 You also don't want any light sources between the viewers and the screen. These light sources can compete with the television display and distract the viewer. You should also avoid any large objects between the listeners and the speakers, which can block the sound.

7 When watching in a darkened room, you need some slight contrast between the bright screen and the dark wall around it. Consider installing a small aquarium-type light behind your television, directed upwards, to provide a halo of soft light around the screen. If the light is too bright, knock it down with a gray or colored filter.

How to Position the Television

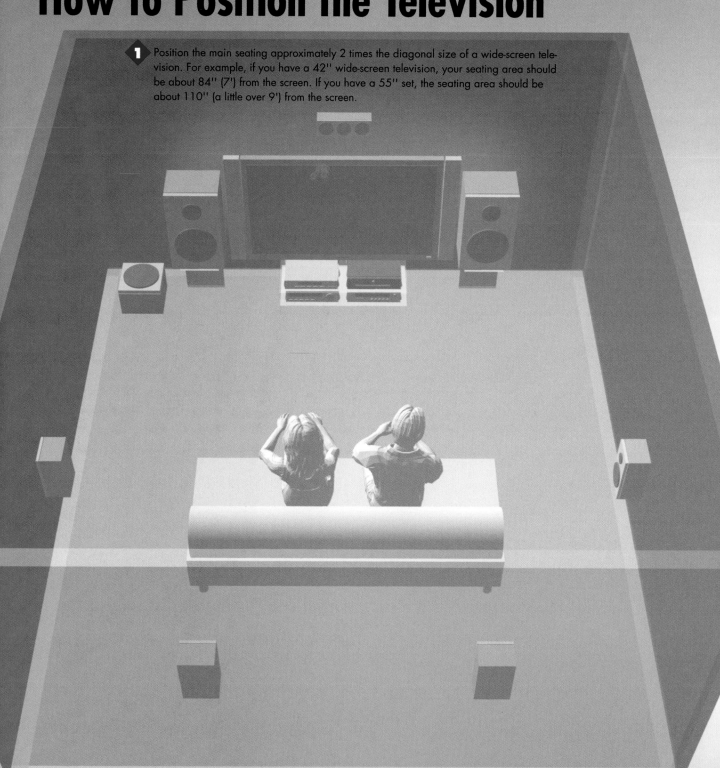

1 Position the main seating approximately 2 times the diagonal size of a wide-screen television. For example, if you have a 42" wide-screen television, your seating area should be about 84" (7') from the screen. If you have a 55" set, the seating area should be about 110" (a little over 9') from the screen.

2 For a CRT rear-projection display, viewer seating should be located within a 90° total angle from the center of the television screen. For a DLP or an LCD rear-projection display, viewer seating should be located within a 130° total angle. For a plasma or an LCD flat-panel display, viewer seating should be located within a 160° total angle. For a CRT direct-view display, viewer seating should be located within a 170° total angle.

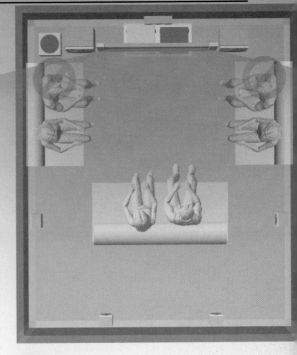

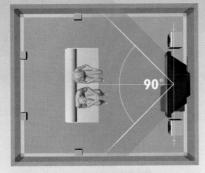

CRT rear projectors

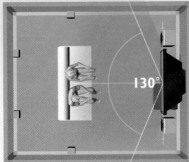

**DLP projector
LCD projector**

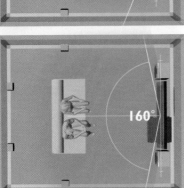

**Plasma panel
LCD panel**

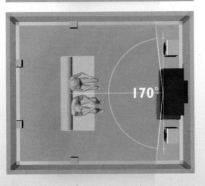

Direct-view CRT

3 Consider all the possible viewing positions within the room. Viewers sitting too close to the screen might notice annoying pixilation or screen door effects. Viewers sitting too far off axis might see a darker picture with some projection and flat-panel technologies. Off-axis problems are minimized the farther away the viewer is from the screen.

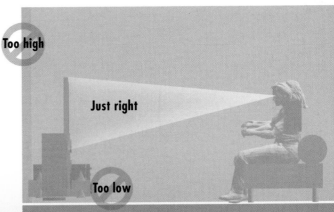

4 The video display should be positioned more or less at eye level. That might mean raising a low-sitting rear-projection set or getting a taller stand for a direct-view monitor. If your display is positioned too high or too low, you risk some off-axis effects (in the form of a darkened or distorted picture) in the horizontal direction. Use the same viewing angle guidelines as for vertical positioning.

How to Position the Speakers

3 Position the center speaker either directly above or directly below the television screen. Above the screen is generally better because a below-the-screen position can result in the speaker pointing at your knees rather than your ears. Try to position the center speaker no more than 12" above or below the midrange or tweeter of the left and right speakers.

Center

1 Try to position all five front and surround speakers at or near the same height. This facilitates the proper positioning of sound elements that move around the theater sound field.

2 The ideal height for all your speakers is ear level (sitting ear level, of course). If you can't get them exactly at ear level, strive for positioning no more than 10° off the horizontal axis.

Surround left

Right front

Left front

Alternative center position

4 The left and right front speakers should be positioned immediately to the left and right of the television screen. Ideally, each speaker should be located between 22° and 30° from the main listening position—even if this means moving them away from the television screen slightly.

8 The subwoofer is nondirectional, so where you put it is unimportant in terms of positioning the sound field. Placing the subwoofer in a corner or under a stairway, however, can add a little extra oomph to your system's low end and should be considered.

5 In a 5.1 or greater system, the surround speakers should be positioned to the left and right sides of the main listening area—not to the rear. You can position these speakers either in line with or slightly behind the listener's ears, between 90° and 110° from the main listening position. Horizontally, both surround speakers should be positioned slightly above ear level—up to 2' above, if possible.

Surround right

7 In a 7.1 system, the two rear speakers should be positioned behind the viewer. One speaker should be slightly to the left and the other slightly to the right, between 135° and 150° from the front of the listener.

Rear L & R (6.1 systems use a single speaker)

6 In a 6.1 system, the single rear speaker should be positioned directly behind the viewer—180° from the front of the listener.

9 The closer a speaker is placed to intersecting room surfaces—a corner, the wall and ceiling, or the wall and floor—the stronger its bass output. This effect can result in overpowering or muddy bass, so unless you deliberately want a bass boost (with a subwoofer, perhaps), keep your speakers away from corners. For the same reason, you should also leave at least 6" between the rear of any speaker and the adjoining wall.

How to Connect the Components

1 Connect the video outputs from each source (DVD player, cable/satellite box, DVR, and so on) to one of the video inputs on the back of the audio/video receiver. Only connect one type of video cable from each component; if multiple connections are offered, use the one that provides the best picture quality.

2 Connect the audio outputs from each source to one of the audio inputs on the back of the audio/video receiver. Only connect one type of audio cable from each component; if multiple connections are offered, use the one that provides the best quality (typically optical or coaxial digital).

3 Connect video outputs from the A/V receiver to your TV. If your receiver upconverts lower-quality formats, you may be able to connect a single cable. (If your receiver upconverts S-Video signals to component video, you make a component video connection without connecting an S-Video cable.) If your receiver doesn't do this, you may need a cable for each type of connection from a source component.

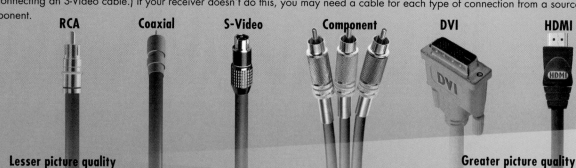

RCA   Coaxial   S-Video   Component   DVI   HDMI

Lesser picture quality   **Greater picture quality**

6 If your television has multiple high-quality video connections (component, DVI, or HDMI), you might want to connect your DVD player and any high-definition source directly, bypassing the A/V receiver for the video connection. A direct connection typically offers slightly better picture quality that might be noticeable on HDTV material.

4 Connect speaker wires from the A/V receiver's speaker outputs to each of your surround sound speakers.

5 Connect an RCA audio cable from the A/V receiver's subwoofer output to the matching input on your subwoofer.

Power Play

Given that your system will include a half-dozen or more components that all need their own power, you'll need to supplement the standard power outlet with a multiple-outlet power strip—preferably one that also functions as a surge suppressor. Look for a surge suppressor with power, RF, and phone line connections because power surges can also come through your antenna, cable, or phone line!

SATELLITE 1

OUT

IN

SATELLITE 2

OUT

IN

ANTENNA OR CABLE TV

OUT

SURGE PROTECTION   GRO

How to Connect the Speakers

1 Use a quality speaker wire. The lower the gauge, the thicker the wire—and thicker wire is better. For example, 10-gauge wire is thicker than 12-gauge. The longer the speaker run, the thicker the wire necessary.

14-gauge

12-gauge

10-gauge

Speaker Wire Guide

Distance run	Recommended gauge speaker wire
<100 feet	14 gauge
100 to 200 feet	12 gauge
>200 feet	10 gauge

Bare wire connects to spring clip speaker terminals.

2 Choose the type of speaker wire connection that is easiest for you and is supported by both your audio/video receiver and your speakers. Your choices typically include bare wire ends (which work with both screw connections and terminal posts), spade connectors (which also work with screws and posts), and banana connectors (which work only with matching banana jacks).

Spade connector works with screws and posts.

Banana plugs work only with matching banana jacks.

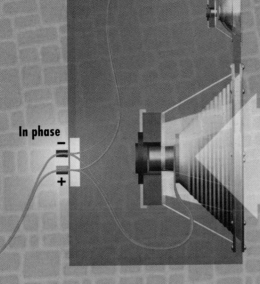

In phase

−
+

−
+

3 Connect the positive (+) and negative (−) leads on your speaker wire the same way at both ends (at the receiver and at the speaker). This ensures that your speakers are all hooked up in phase.

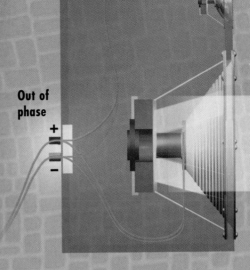

Out of phase

+
−

4 If you find that your speakers are out of phase—that is, if the cone from one speaker is moving out while the cone on another speaker is moving in—you can bring them back in phase by reversing the leads for one of the speakers.

Single RCA cable

Power cable

5 The subwoofer is not connected via speaker wire. This is because the subwoofer contains its own built-in amplifier. The connection to the subwoofer is made via a single RCA audio cable. Shielded cable is better for longer runs.

How to Calibrate the Picture

1 Begin by placing all the controls on your television set into the manual or normal settings. You want to avoid the "showroom" or "demo" settings that typically boost brightness and color to levels unacceptable for living room use.

3 Adjust the brightness and contrast controls until you see deep blacks without losing detail in the shadows. These two controls work in conjunction with each other to adjust the white and black levels of your picture.

2 Turn the color or saturation control all the way down until you have a black-and-white picture.

4 Adjust the sharpness control to achieve sufficient detail without introducing grain or video noise.

Professional Calibration

For more sophisticated picture calibration, obtain a copy of the DVD *AVIA Guide to Home Theater*. This disc contains dozens of tests and routines to help you fine-tune your picture calibration. You can also use a professional technician to perform these same high-level adjustments.

5 Turn up the color or saturation control until the color level is natural and vivid without being excessive or "blooming."

6 Adjust the tint or hue control until skin tones look natural.

7 To introduce a slight orange or reddish cast to white areas of the picture, adjust the color temperature control to the "warm" setting. To introduce a slight bluish cast to white areas of the picture, adjust the color temperature control to the "cool" setting. Otherwise, leave this control in the neutral position.

How to Calibrate the Sound

```
SET UP - DSP MODES
1 OFF
2 Cinema
3 Concert Hall
4 Auditorium
5 Stadium

> next item      adjust <->
  MENU - DSP Modes
```

1 On your audio/video receiver, turn off all digital signal processing (DSP) modes and go directly to the speaker setup or configuration menu.

```
SET UP SPEAKER SIZE
1 Front              Small
2 Center             Small
3 Surround           Small
4 Surround Back      Small
5 Subwoofer          Yes

> next item      adjust <->
  MENU - Setup Speakers
```

3 If necessary, turn on your receiver's LFE or bass management feature. (This is turned on by default on most A/V receivers.) This can be as simple as selecting Yes for the subwoofer in the speaker size menu.

```
SET UP SPEAKER SIZE
1 Front              Small
2 Center             Small
3 Surround           Small
4 Surround Back      Small
5 Subwoofer          Yes

> next item      adjust <->
  MENU - Setup Speakers
```

2 Unless you're using large, floor-standing speakers, set the size setting for each of your speakers to Small. (You should use the Large setting only if your speakers have large woofers.)

```
SPEAKER LOCATION - in feet
             Left   Center  Right
Front        10.0   10.0    10.0
Surround     10.0   -       10.0
Back         10.0   -       10.0
Subwoofer -         10.0    -

> next item      adjust <->
  MENU - Setup Speakers
```

4 Measure the distance from your main listening position to each speaker, and then enter this distance for each speaker in the setup menu.

```
SPEAKER LOCATION - in feet
            Left   Center  Right
Front       0.0db  0.0db   0.0db
Surround    0.0db    -     0.0db
Back        0.0db    -     0.0db
Subwoofer     -    0.0db     -

> next item        adjust <->
MENU - Setup Speakers
```

Professional Calibration

For more sophisticated calibration, you'll need a sound pressure level (SPL) meter and the DVD AVIA *Guide to Home Theater*. You can use the SPL meter to precisely measure the sound level from each of your speakers per the *AVIA* disc's tests and then make appropriate adjustments on your receiver.

5 Run your receiver's sound level test, which plays a burst of pink noise through each channel, successively. Adjust the sound level for each speaker until they sound equal to you. (Note that many listeners typically run the center and surround speakers too loud; you want a balanced sound across all the speakers.)

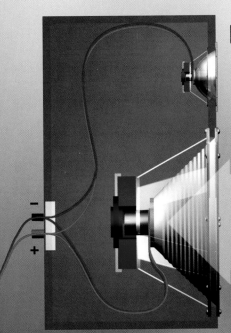

In phase

6 While you're running the sound level test, listen for the pitch of the pink noise from each speaker. If one channel sounds noticeably lower in pitch than the others, it might be connected out of phase; check the polarity of that speaker's connections to correct this.

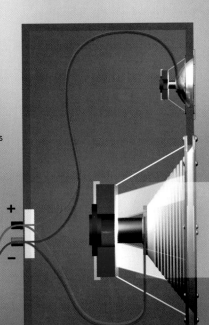

Out of phase

CHAPTER
20

How Video Cables Work

BEFORE there was home theater and all these fancy components, you only had to deal with a flat antenna wire or coax cable to your TV, plugging a right/left audio cable between your turntable and your receiver (remember turntables?), and running speaker wire to all two of your speakers. There weren't a ton of extra components to worry about, nor was there any connection between your TV and your stereo system. Life was simpler then.

Now, even the least expensive home theater system forces you to deal with six or more speakers, a variety of audio and video components, and a number of different connection options. Life is more complicated. (Well, at least you don't have to worry about connecting a turntable anymore!)

Before you try plugging anything in, it's probably a good idea to understand all these types of connections—and when to use which ones. In general, when faced with a choice of connections, you should use the connection that offers the highest-quality audio or video. This requires you to have a working knowledge of the various connection types, from familiar old coax to the latest component and HDMI video connections. (And it's not just video that's confusing; those good old RCA audio cables have been augmented by newer optical and coaxial digital cables.)

When given the choice of connections, choose the one that offers the best audio/video quality. In general, digital connections are better than analog ones, and connections that separate the various parts of a signal are better than those that smoosh everything together into a single feed.

For video, this means HDMI or DVI digital connections are better than any of the analog choices, if you have that choice. Within the analog world, component video connections (which use three separate cables) are superior to the other choices, and S-Video (which separates the color information from the brightness information) is better than composite video (which doesn't separate anything). In addition, if you're dealing with high-definition video, you'll need to get at least component video cables; lower-quality connections can't carry the HD signal. And for audio, optical and coaxial digital connections are far superior to the traditional line audio and RCA connections.

Higher-quality components require higher-quality connections. If you're connecting a progressive scan DVD player or a high-definition video source (such as a HD cable or satellite set-top box), you'll need to use either component video cables or a DVI or HDMI connection. If you're connecting a next-generation Blu-ray Disc or HD DVD player, you have to use an HDMI connection, which will carry both video and audio signals.

You also need to consider the length of your cables. Too-long cable runs increase the possibility of signal leakage and degradation, as well as interference from outside sources. Keep your cables and wires as short as possible; leave just enough extra to comfortably pull out your components to access the rear panels. What you don't want to do is use cables several feet longer than necessary—and then leave the excess wadded up or rolled up behind your system!

How Coaxial Connections Work

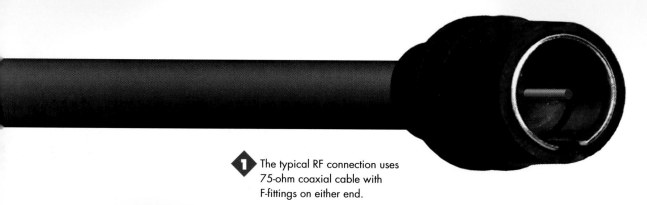

1 The typical RF connection uses 75-ohm coaxial cable with F-fittings on either end.

2 The signal is carried through the copper wire in the middle of the cable. The wire is shielded from interference by an aluminum foil wrap.

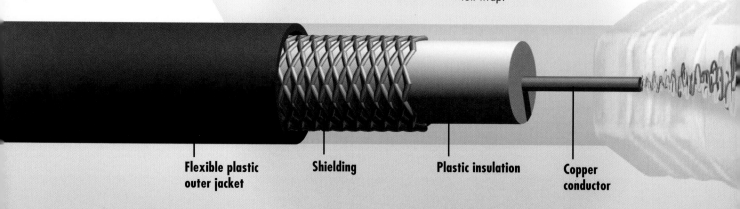

Flexible plastic outer jacket   **Shielding**   **Plastic insulation**   **Copper conductor**

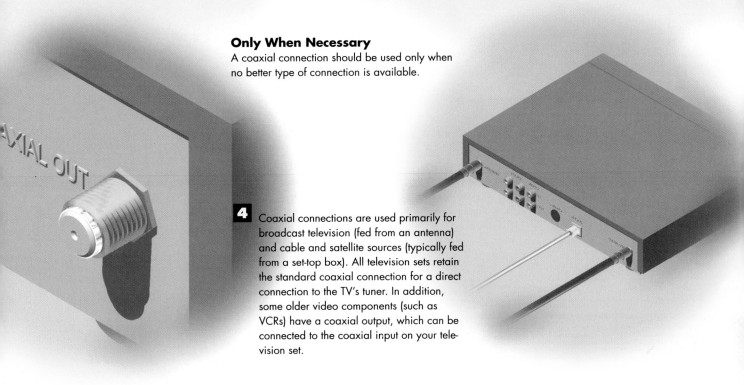

Only When Necessary
A coaxial connection should be used only when no better type of connection is available.

4 Coaxial connections are used primarily for broadcast television (fed from an antenna) and cable and satellite sources (typically fed from a set-top box). All television sets retain the standard coaxial connection for a direct connection to the TV's tuner. In addition, some older video components (such as VCRs) have a coaxial output, which can be connected to the coaxial input on your television set.

3 A coaxial cable transmits an RF (radio frequency) signal that carries both audio and video information all mixed together. Unfortunately, RF is less precise in separating chrominance and luminance than other technologies, resulting in a noticeably less-sharp picture with poor color separation.

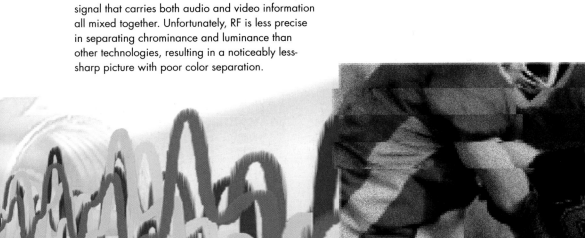

Video (color and brightness) information is mixed together with audio information.

How Composite Video Connections Work

Standard connectors

1 A composite video connection uses a standard RCA plug and jack, typically in a shielded cable. (The shielding is necessary to prevent visible degradation of the video signal.)

Gold-plated connectors

2 Unlike an RF connection, a composite video connection carries only video signals. (Audio signals have to be transmitted via separate line audio connections.) The composite video signal contains both chrominance (color) and luminance (brightness) information.

Flexible plastic outer jacket **Shielding** **Flexible insulation** **Copper conductor**

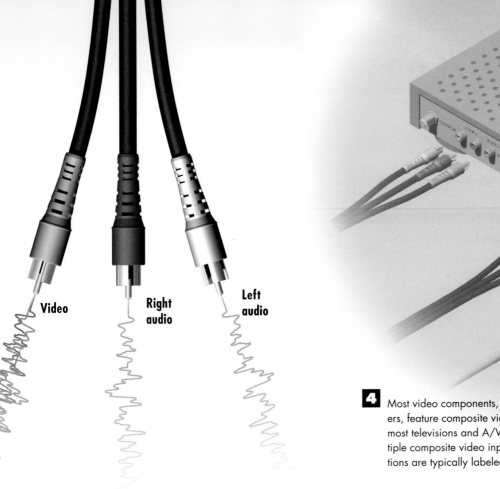

Video

Right
audio

Left
audio

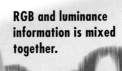

4 Most video components, such as DVD players, feature composite video outputs, and
most televisions and A/V receivers have multiple composite video inputs. These connections are typically labeled just "video."

RGB and luminance
information is mixed
together.

3 A composite video signal is higher quality
than an RF (coaxial) signal but not as sharp
or vivid as the signal carried by an S-Video
or component video cable.

Picture quality is improved over RF coaxial.

How S-Video Connections Work

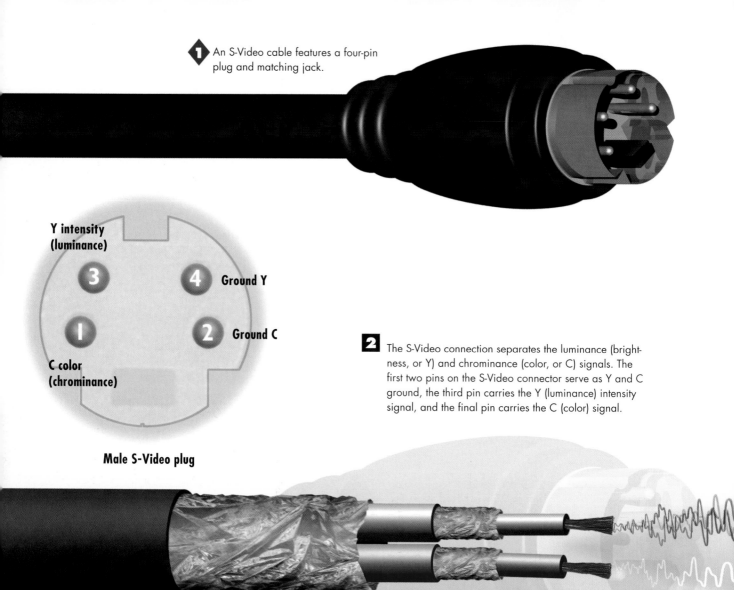

1 An S-Video cable features a four-pin plug and matching jack.

Y intensity (luminance)

3

4 Ground Y

1

2 Ground C

C color (chrominance)

Male S-Video plug

2 The S-Video connection separates the luminance (brightness, or Y) and chrominance (color, or C) signals. The first two pins on the S-Video connector serve as Y and C ground, the third pin carries the Y (luminance) intensity signal, and the final pin carries the C (color) signal.

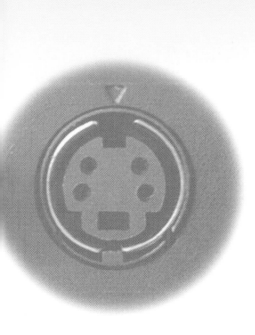

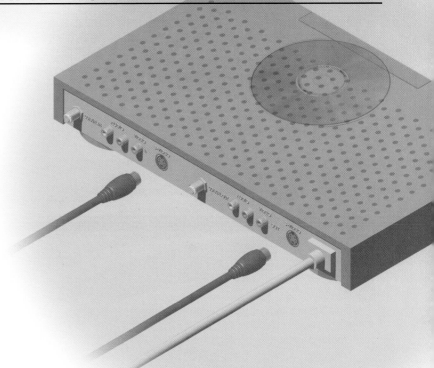

4 Most video components, televisions, and A/V receivers utilize S-Video connections. An S-Video connection is preferred to a simple "video" (composite video) or coaxial connection.

Chrominance

Luminance

3 By separating the luminance and chrominance information, an S-Video connection delivers a sharper picture with improved color accuracy and reduced distortion than either RF (coaxial) or composite video connections.

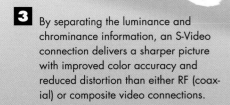

Better picture quality than coaxial or composite

How Component Video Connections Work

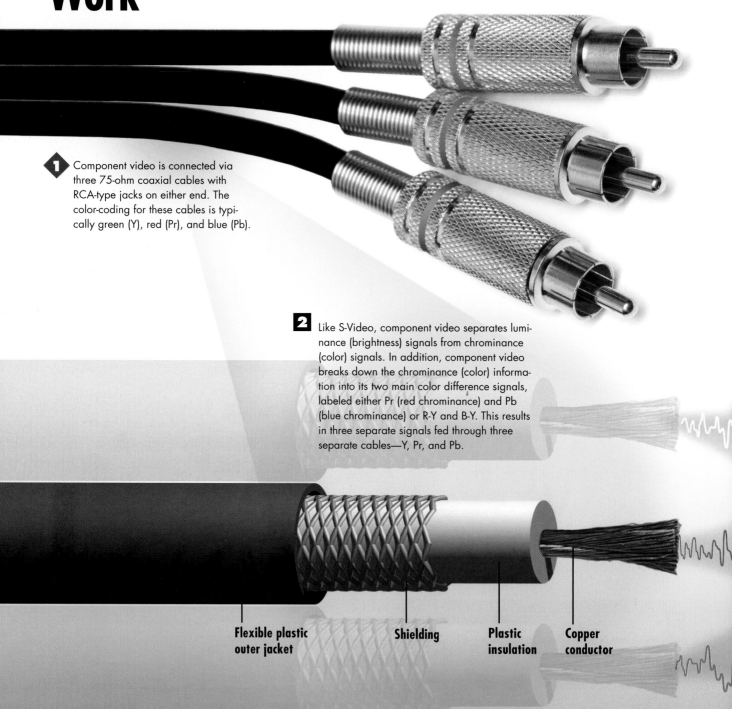

1 Component video is connected via three 75-ohm coaxial cables with RCA-type jacks on either end. The color-coding for these cables is typically green (Y), red (Pr), and blue (Pb).

2 Like S-Video, component video separates luminance (brightness) signals from chrominance (color) signals. In addition, component video breaks down the chrominance (color) information into its two main color difference signals, labeled either Pr (red chrominance) and Pb (blue chrominance) or R-Y and B-Y. This results in three separate signals fed through three separate cables—Y, Pr, and Pb.

Flexible plastic outer jacket

Shielding

Plastic insulation

Copper conductor

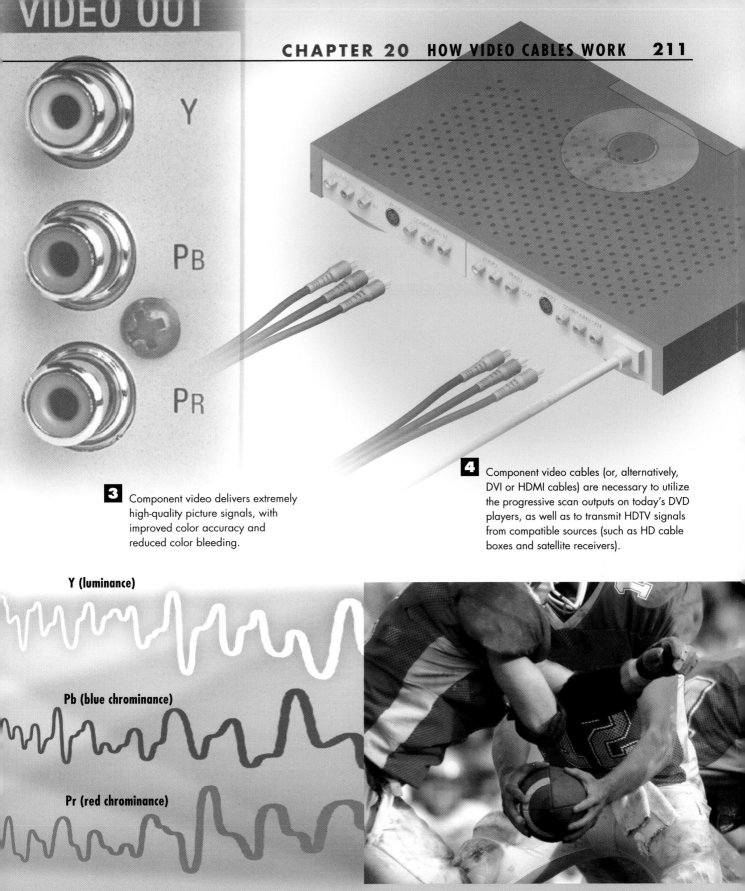

3 Component video delivers extremely high-quality picture signals, with improved color accuracy and reduced color bleeding.

4 Component video cables (or, alternatively, DVI or HDMI cables) are necessary to utilize the progressive scan outputs on today's DVD players, as well as to transmit HDTV signals from compatible sources (such as HD cable boxes and satellite receivers).

Y (luminance)

Pb (blue chrominance)

Pr (red chrominance)

How DVI Connections Work

1 A Digital Visual Interface (DVI) connection is a digital connection, as opposed to the previous analog connections. The DVI cable uses a 24-pin connector, with three rows of 8 pins each. (Some variations of the DVI standard use more or fewer pins, but the 24-pin arrangement is the default for home video use.)

There are actually several types of DVI connections. DVI-D transmits pure digital-to-digital signals and is used in HD home theaters. DVI-A transmits high-resolution analog-to-analog signals. DVI-I can transmit either digital-to-digital or analog-to-analog signals. DVI-I and DVD-D connections are available in Single-Link and Dual-Link formats; a Dual-Link cable can transmit twice the data as a comparable Single-Link cable.

 **DVI-I Single Link**

 **DVI-A Single Link (analog only)**

 **DVI-D Single Link (digital only)**

 **DVI-I Dual Link (analog and digital)**

DVI-D Dual Link (digital only)

2 DVI carries video signals in pure digital form, offering superior video quality to any of the previous analog connections, including component video. By using a DVI cable, you create an uncompressed, unaltered digital-to-digital connection that eliminates any connection to analog format—and the resulting deterioration in picture quality.

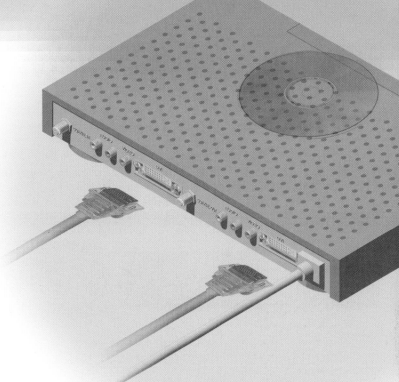

4 DVI is typically used to connect LCD computer monitors to PCs and to connect high-end DVD players and high-definition cable boxes and satellite receivers. Not all televisions have DVI connections; many manufacturers are bypassing DVI in favor of the newer HDMI digital connection.

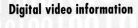

Digital video information

3 Digital video signals transmitted via DVI can be encrypted with High-bandwidth Digital Content Protection (HDCP) to prevent unauthorized recording.

Better picture quality than coaxial or composite

How HDMI Connections Work

1 A High definition multimedia interface (HDMI) connection is like a DVI digital video connection that also carries digital audio. An HDMI cable uses a 19-pin connector that is smaller and sleeker than the older DVI connector.

2 Because HDMI carries uncompressed digital data, it has the same picture quality as DVI—which is superior to any analog connection. It has a bandwidth of 5Gb per second.

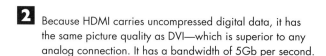

DVI to HDMI
Because many newer devices are coming with only HDMI connections (no DVI), some manufacturers make DVI-to-HDMI connectors. These enable you to connect a DVI device to an HDMI display.

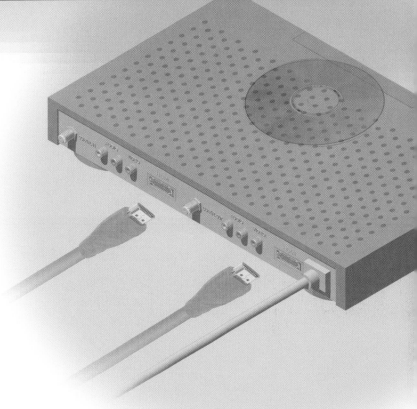

4 Like DVI, HDMI video signals can be encrypted with High-bandwidth Digital Content Protection (HDCP) to prevent unauthorized recording.

5 HDMI connectors can be found on some higher-end cable and satellite boxes, DVD players, A/V receivers, and high-definition television displays.

Better picture quality than coaxial or composite

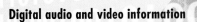
Digital audio and video information

3 When you use an HDMI connection, you don't have to make a separate audio connection between your two devices. The HDMI cable can carry up to eight channels of digital audio, which means it can handle the 7.1-channel soundtracks of Dolby Digital EX.

Audio + Video

How Different Video Connections Compare

Overall video performance

Connection	Cable/Connector	Analog or Digital?	Signals Carried	Quality
HDMI	Slim 19-pin connector	Digital	Digital video (HDTV quality) plus separate digital audio signals	Best
DVI	Large 28-pin connector	Digital (DVI-I or DVI-D)	Digital video only (HDTV quality)	Best
Component video	Three shielded cables (green, red, blue) with RCA jacks	Analog	Video only; separate luminance, red chrominance, and blue chrominance	Better
S-Video	Shielded cable with 4-pin connector	Analog	Video only; separate luminance and chrominance	Good
Composite video	Shielded cable with RCA jacks	Analog	Video only; luminance and chrominance mixed together	Acceptable
RF	Coaxial cable with F-fittings	Analog	Video and audio (mixed together)	Poor

Video Connection Preference

If you're not sure which video connections to use, just remember to use the highest-quality connections first, if available. Here's the order in which you want to choose your connections:

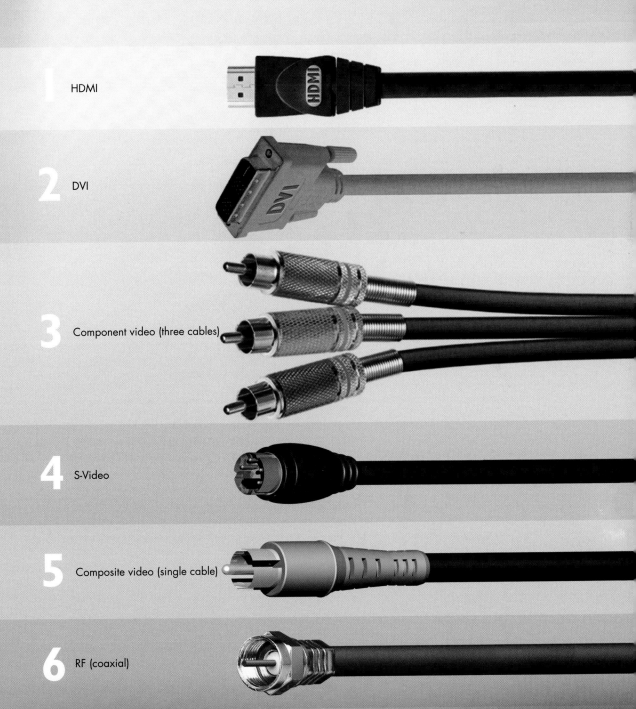

1 HDMI

2 DVI

3 Component video (three cables)

4 S-Video

5 Composite video (single cable)

6 RF (coaxial)

CHAPTER

21

How Audio Cables Work

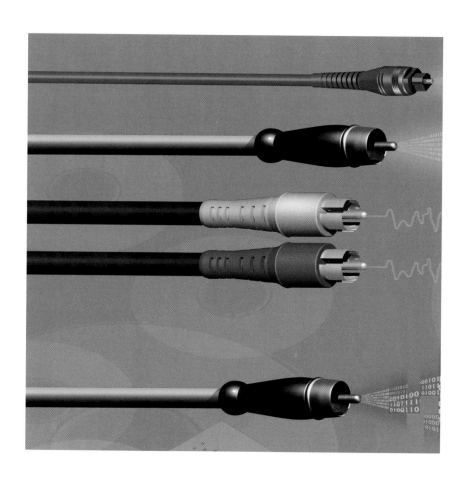

AUDIO connections aren't quite as complex as video connections because audio signals are easier to transmit than video signals—sort of. After all, for decades we only had to deal with two channels of audio: right and left. What could be simpler than that? (Well, monophonic audio, of course, but we haven't had that since the 1950s....)

With the advent of surround sound, however, the audio situation became more complex. All of a sudden there developed the need to transmit six or more channels of audio. How to do it?

The simplest solution was to simply add four more RCA audio connections. And, in fact, that's how early surround sound components were connected—with multiple RCA audio cables. That worked, but it wasn't very efficient.

It also wasn't the best possible quality. That's because traditional RCA audio cables carry analog audio signals, and analog signals aren't as good as digital signals. And, after all, Dolby Digital Surround Sound is digital to start with—why move back into the analog world when you have to connect two components?

The solution to this situation was the invention of the digital audio connection, sometimes called an S/PDIF connection (for Sony/Philips Digital Interface). This is a single cable that can carry multiple channels of audio in pure digital form—very efficient, and very high quality. Today we have two types of digital audio cables to choose from: coaxial and optical. Both offer similar sound quality, but each has its pros and cons. It's hard to go wrong with either one, though.

In addition, the new HDMI connection covered in Chapter 20, "How Video Cables Work," is capable of carrying both digital video and audio. If you connect your components via HDMI, you don't need to make a separate audio connection—it's all there in the single HDMI cable. Just connect the HDMI cable to your A/V receiver; the video will be passed through to your television set, and the receiver will process the digital surround sound audio.

Using HDMI is just an option with today's high-end audio/video equipment, but it will be required to carry the digital surround-sound audio from new high-definition DVD formats. Dolby Digital TrueHD and DTS HD use higher bit rates than standard Dolby Digital and DTS, and today's optical and coaxial digital cables don't have enough bandwidth for these future surround-sound standards. (S/PDIF has a data transfer rate of 1.5MB per second, whereas HDMI transfers data at a blazing 5GB per second!) For this reason, HDMI will be the connection of choice for both Blu-ray Disc and HD DVD players.

How Line Audio Connections Work

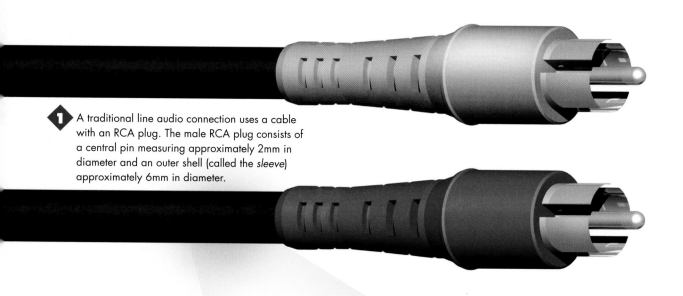

1 A traditional line audio connection uses a cable with an RCA plug. The male RCA plug consists of a central pin measuring approximately 2mm in diameter and an outer shell (called the *sleeve*) approximately 6mm in diameter.

2 The audio signals are carried a copper wire surrounded by an insulating PVC jacket. The wire feeds a positive electrical current to the pin of the connector, while the sleeve serves as a shield or ground.

Shielding

Flexible insulation

Copper conductor

Flexible plastic outer jacket

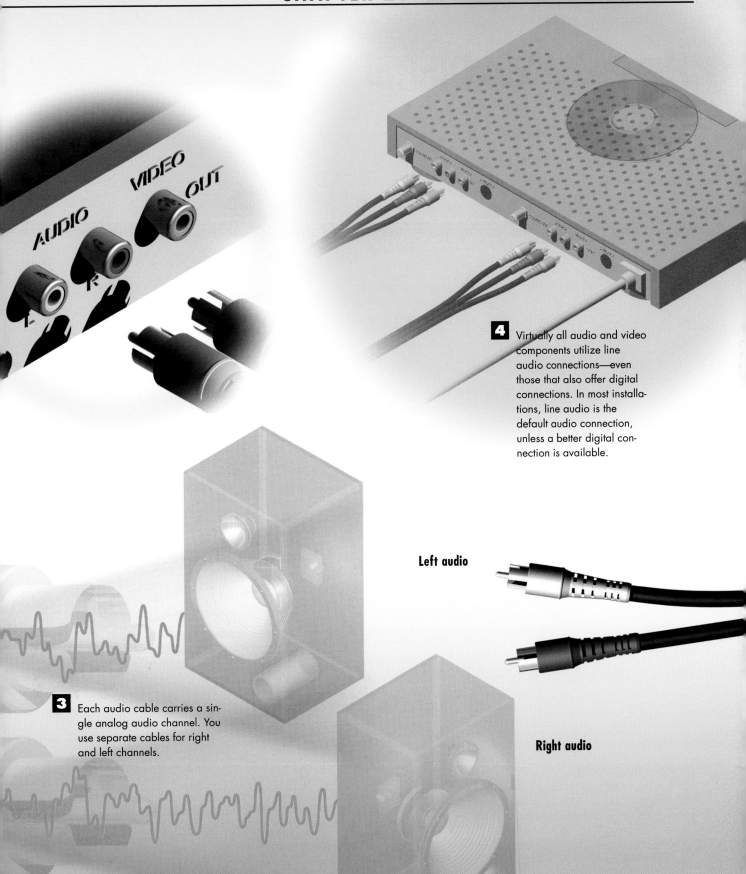

4 Virtually all audio and video components utilize line audio connections—even those that also offer digital connections. In most installations, line audio is the default audio connection, unless a better digital connection is available.

Left audio

Right audio

3 Each audio cable carries a single analog audio channel. You use separate cables for right and left channels.

How Optical Digital Connections Work

1 An optical digital cable transmits a digital audio signal across a fiber-optic cable. The connectors at either end of the digital optical cable are called Toslink or EIA-J connectors.

2 The fiber-optic cable consists of several small strands of polished plastic specifically designed to transfer light. Because you don't need to shield an optical signal, optical digital cables are thinner than coaxial digital cables.

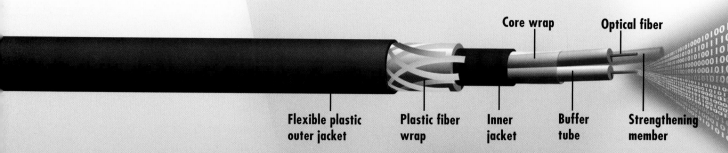

Core wrap   **Optical fiber**

Flexible plastic outer jacket   **Plastic fiber wrap**   **Inner jacket**   **Buffer tube**   **Strengthening member**

Beware the Bends!
The only drawback to using an optical digital cable is that the signal can sometimes be affected by extreme bends in the cable. You can't get light to turn corners!

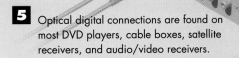

5 Optical digital connections are found on most DVD players, cable boxes, satellite receivers, and audio/video receivers.

3 The digital audio signals are transmitted through the cable as pulses of light. These light pulses are immune to electrical interference, and the signal holds up extremely well over long distances.

4 The optical cable carries the entire digital bitstream—as many channels as your two components can utilize. The result is improved sound quality when compared to traditional line audio connections.

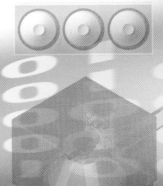

**Fiber-optic cables have
enough bandwidth to handle
7.1 audio and more!**

How Coaxial Digital Connections Work

1 ▶ The other primary type of digital audio connection is the coaxial digital connection, which transmits the digital signal electrically through copper wire. Visually, a digital coaxial cable looks like a coaxial cable with RCA connectors on each end.

2 Digital coax transmits signals electrically. The electrical signal pulses through the copper wire at the heart of the coaxial cable. It is shielded from interference by an aluminum foil wrap.

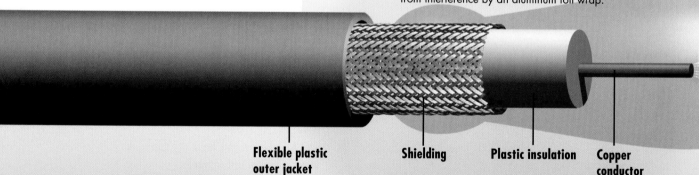

Flexible plastic outer jacket   **Shielding**   **Plastic insulation**   **Copper conductor**

Watch the Length
As good as digital coaxial cable is, there are some inherent problems with the format, chiefly due to the limitations of the electrical signal. Electrical signals degrade over long distances (around 50 feet) and are prone to interference from other electrical devices—even when shielded, as with coaxial cable.

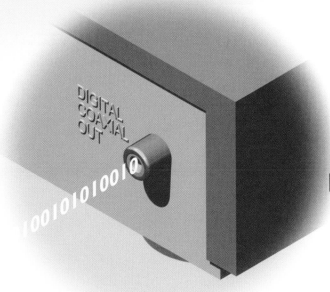

4 Digital coaxial connections are found on most DVD players, cable boxes, satellite receivers, and audio/video receivers.

3 The digital coaxial cable carries the entire digital bitstream—as many channels as your two components can utilize. The result is improved sound quality when compared to traditional line audio connections.

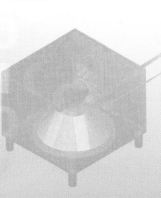

Digital audio channels

How Different Audio Connections Compare

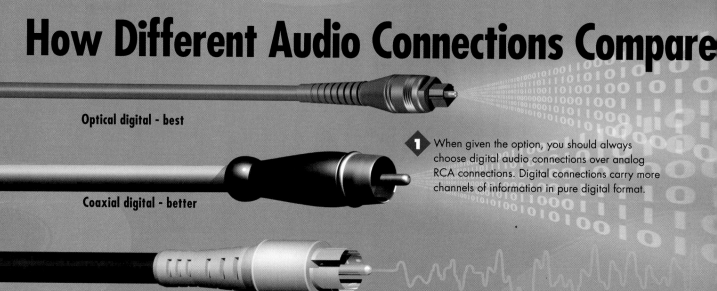

Optical digital - best

Coaxial digital - better

Analog composite - acceptable

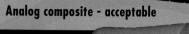

1 When given the option, you should always choose digital audio connections over analog RCA connections. Digital connections carry more channels of information in pure digital format.

2 Because optical digital cables are less susceptible than coaxial digital cables to electrical interference, these cables are a good choice if you have a lot of "noisy" electrical devices in the same area.

3 Coaxial digital cables are bit a more rugged than optical digital cables and provide a tighter fit, thanks to the use of RCA jacks. If your equipment is often moved or prone to jostling, coaxial cables are a better choice.

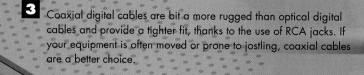

4 Because light waves don't turn corners, optical connections are not recommended for complex cabling situations. Instead, you should use coaxial cables when you have to make tight bends around corners.

5 Optical digital cables are slimmer than coaxial cables, which might matter if space is at a premium.

6 Optical digital cables have less signal loss than coaxial cables and are better for longer runs. If you have to run cable farther than 50 feet or so, go with an optical digital cable.

CHAPTER

22

How Remote Controls Work

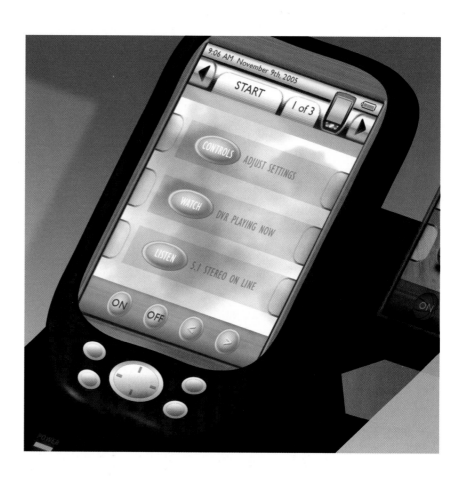

A home theater system consists of many components—a television set, an audio/video receiver, a DVD player, a DVR, and maybe even a media center PC and video game console. Each of these components is operated by its own proprietary remote control unit, which means you end up with a half-dozen or so remotes cluttering your coffee table. What can you do about this remote control clutter?

The solution to this problem is a single remote control that operates multiple components. By consolidating all the functions into a single unit, you can put all the individual remotes in the closet and forget about them. The challenge, however, is choosing the best single remote for all your system needs.

You can choose from three types of multiple-unit remote controls:

- **Universal** remote controls come preprogrammed with operating codes for multiple components from multiple manufacturers.

- **Learning** remotes "learn" the operating codes from your existing remotes.

- **Programmable** remotes typically include some combination of preprogrammed codes and learning capabilities but then let you program in your own multiple-step functions (via automated *macros*) and configure your own remote control interface on a built-in LCD screen.

All three types of remotes operate multiple components but differ in how easy they are to set up and operate. A universal remote is arguably the easiest type of remote to get up and running; programmable remotes require much more upfront work, but they can make any complex operation pretty much a one-button affair.

The choice isn't always clear-cut, however, because some remotes blend features from these different general types. For example, it's not unusual to find learning remotes that include universal codes, or programmable remotes that include both universal and learning functions. And then there's price. Universal remotes are fairly inexpensive, while programmable remotes can cost anywhere up to $1,000. (You might also be able to get by with the remote that comes with your A/V receiver, which typically offers some universal or learning functions.) So choose carefully—and make sure that the remote you choose can operate all the components you use!

Most remote control units designed for livingroom use transmit their signals via infrared light. As long as you have a clear line of sight between the remote unit and your A/V components, the remote should work fine. Infrared does not work well, however, when components are stored in a closed cabinet or in another room. For these situations, a radio frequency (RF) remote is recommended because RF signals can transmit through walls and other solid objects.

Finally, some high-end home theater systems employ custom-designed remote control interfaces. These remotes typically use a large touch-panel LCD control that has been programmed to control all aspects of the home theater experience, as well as other home automation, such as closing curtains and dimming lights. These remote systems are expensive and have to be custom-programmed by an authorized installer. It's the ultimate way to go!

How Infrared Remotes Work

1 As the name implies, an infrared remote control operates via a beam of infrared light. This means that the component you're trying to operate must be in line of sight with the remote unit to receive the signals. (Infrared remotes can't operate components in other rooms because light beams can't penetrate walls.)

2 The remote transmits pulses of infrared light in the 30KHz–40KHz frequency range. The pulses of infrared light are used to send operating codes to the source component. Since the light can only be on or off, the code must be binary—a series of 1s (on) and 0s (off). The code can also incorporate different lengths of pulses and of the spaces between pulses.

3 When a button on the remote is first pushed, it transmits a header string that alerts all infrared receivers in the area that a string of data is being sent.

Header string   004   004   004   0

4 Following the header string is the operating code itself, called a *command*. As long as the button on the remote is depressed, the command continues to repeat.

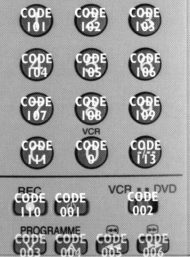

6 There are separate codes for each key function on the component. For example, a television set has dozens of commands—for volume up, volume down, channel up, channel down, and for each number you use to select a channel directly.

Infrared Blasters

One common home theater accessory is the *infrared blaster*. This is a small, bug-like device that attaches to the front of one component and the back of another and sends infrared remote control signals from the second unit to control the operation of the first. Infrared blasters are used when one component needs to control another. For example, if you want your DVR to control your cable box (to record a program when you're away), you attach the DVR's infrared blaster to the front of your cable box. The receiver then sends the proper remote control signals to turn on the cable box and tune it to the desired channel, just as if you were sending the signals from a standard remote control.

Stop code

5 When the button on the remote is released, a string of *stop code* is transmitted. This code tells the component to stop executing the command.

How RF Remotes Work

1 When you want to operate components in another room or in a closed cabinet, infrared transmission won't do the job. In these instances, you want a radio frequency (RF) remote, which sends its commands via radio waves instead of light waves.

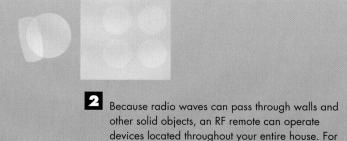

2 Because radio waves can pass through walls and other solid objects, an RF remote can operate devices located throughout your entire house. For this reason, RF remotes are preferred for whole-house and multiple-room installations.

Stop code   Code 1C

4 For an RF remote to work, the source component must be capable of receiving RF signals. Most components are designed for infrared remote operation, so you might need to connect a receiver/converter device to the source component. This is a small device that receives the RF signal and then converts it to infrared; the converted infrared signal is then beamed (via an emitter or IR "bug") to the IR receiver on the front of the source component.

RF receiver connects to IR "bugs" to control multiple components

Code 101   Code 101   Code 101   Code 101   Code 101   Code 101   Code 101

3 An RF remote generates a signal at a given radio frequency, typically in the 300MHz–500MHz range. This frequency is modulated into a series of pulses, much like the pulses used by infrared remotes. These pulses contain the codes for each of the commands sent by the remote.

How Universal Remotes Work

1 To keep different remotes from interfering with each other, the consumer electronics industry has worked out a special set of codes that identify the make and model of component that is being controlled. This keeps your TV remote from starting up your DVD player, and vice versa. Universal remotes work by allowing multiple different codes to be sent from the same remote, so that you can use one device to control all your components.

2 A universal remote control contains a huge database of preprogrammed infrared codes for most popular types and brands of equipment. This database of codes is either hard-coded on a computer memory chip or downloaded (by the remote's manufacturer) to built-in flash memory.

Configuring the Codes

Most universal remotes come with a code sheet that lists most of the codes stored on that remote. In many cases, the remote can control even more components than are listed because new codes are being added every day. If you can't find a code for a particular component, call the remote's manufacturer for an updated code list; if the remote stores its codes in flash memory, you might be able to reprogram the remote with additional codes.

3 To program the remote for a specific component, you punch in the three- or four-digit code number of the unit you want to control. The universal remote then automatically configures itself with the proper operating codes for that component.

de 614
ver - mfgr
43662)

code 8190
(DVD - mfgr
#31298)

code 2176
(audio CD - mfgr
#947256)

code 8741
(pre-amp - mfgr
#1144621)

code 1138
(DVR - mfgr
#7787124)

code 420
(tuner - mfgr
#1481694)

4 Universal remotes can typically control anywhere from three to six components. You switch between components by pressing the appropriate dedicated button on the remote. After a particular component is selected, all the buttons on the remote are used to operate that component. When a button is pressed, the proper IR command for that component is sent.

How Learning Remotes Work

1 A learning remote doesn't rely on preprogrammed codes to operate different components. Instead, a learning remote "learns" the codes directly from the component's standard remote control and can thus work with virtually any audio/video component—even obscure brands and older models.

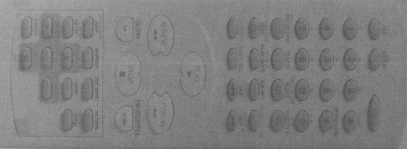

2 To start the learning process, place the component's original remote head-to-head with the learning remote.

3 Press the appropriate button or series of buttons on the learning remote to put it into learning mode.

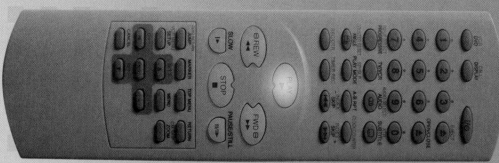

5 While holding down the button on the original remote, press and hold the corresponding button on the learning remote. This enables the learning remote to receive the correct infrared command, store it in memory, and associate it with the depressed button.

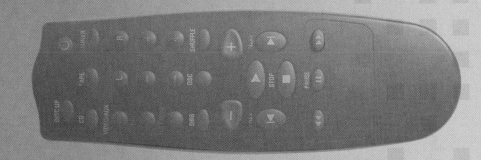

4 On the original
remote, press and hold
the button for the oper-
ation you want the
new remote to learn.

6 After the learning remote
has learned the operation,
it will send a signal—
either by flashing or
beeping—to tell you that
it's done. You can then
release all the buttons and
proceed to program
another operation.

7 After the remote has learned all
the commands from the original
remote, you can use it to operate
the original component.

How Programmable Remotes Work

1 A programmable remote typically includes built-in codes (like a universal remote) and learning functions (like a learning remote) but offers even more programmability that lets you perform operations that involve more than one component in your system. Most programmable remotes incorporate an LCD touch screen; the macro commands you create can be assigned to virtual buttons on the touch screen.

2 To program multiple-component operations, a programming remote lets you create macro commands. A macro incorporates several individual commands, strung together and assigned to a single button.

For example, you could create a "play movie" macro by stringing together the following sequence of commands:
1. Turn on A/V receiver.
2. Switch A/V receiver to DVD input.
3. Turn on TV.
4. Switch TV to DVD input.
5. Turn on DVD player.
6. Press Play on DVD player.

These six commands are then assigned to a single "Play Movie" button on the remote control. When the "Play Movie" button is pressed, the six commands are executed in sequence, which turns on the appropriate components and readies them to play a DVD movie.

9:06 AM November 9th, 2005
START   1 of 3
CONTROLS ADJUST SETTINGS
WATCH DVR PLAYING NOW
LISTEN 5.1 STEREO ON LINE
ON OFF
POWER
IN USE

Turn on A/V receiver + Switch A/V receiver to DVD input + Turn on TV + Switch TV to DVD input + Turn on DVD

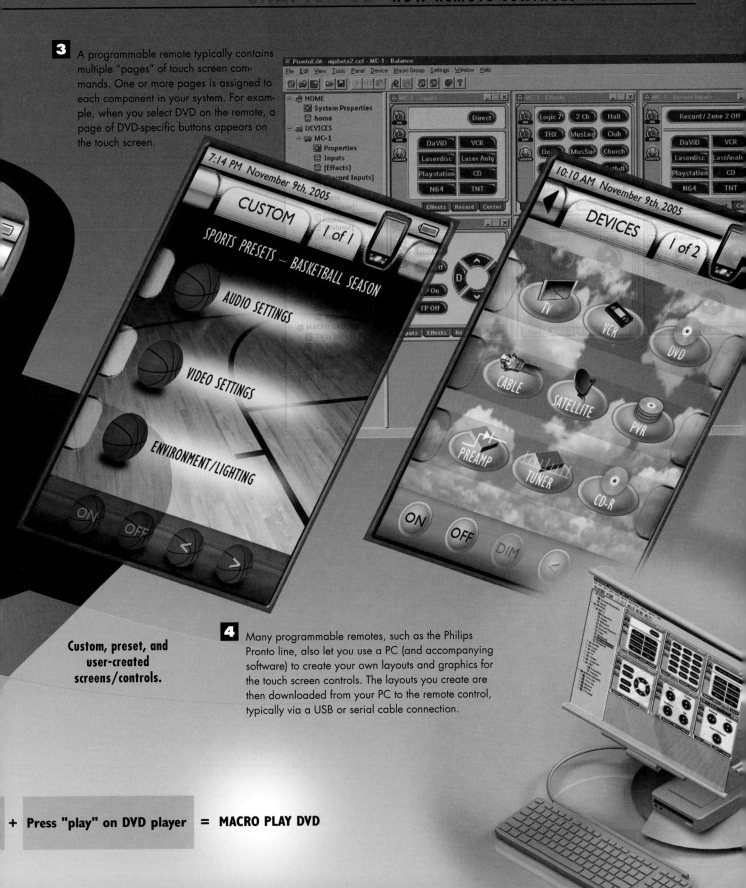

3 A programmable remote typically contains multiple "pages" of touch screen commands. One or more pages is assigned to each component in your system. For example, when you select DVD on the remote, a page of DVD-specific buttons appears on the touch screen.

Custom, preset, and user-created screens/controls.

4 Many programmable remotes, such as the Philips Pronto line, also let you use a PC (and accompanying software) to create your own layouts and graphics for the touch screen controls. The layouts you create are then downloaded from your PC to the remote control, typically via a USB or serial cable connection.

+ **Press "play" on DVD player** = **MACRO PLAY DVD**

How Two-Way Remotes Work

1 Many audio/video components send status information via infrared. For example, a DVD player might send a code that indicates that it is in playback mode, as well as which track is being played. An A/V receiver might send a code that indicates which component is selected, as well as the current volume level.

Power on receiver, power on CD jukebox: select disk 1: play track 3

3 In addition, most two-way remotes incorporate discrete "on" and "off" codes for most components. A regular consumer remote will only send a single "on/off" pulse that toggles the component between on and off modes. By using a discrete code, a two-way remote can (1) sense the current mode (on or off) of the component and then (2) send the appropriate "on" or "off" command as directed. This is a valuable feature when programming complex macros. If you send an "on/off" toggle code to a component that's already on, you'll turn it off; if you use a discrete "on" code, instead, you won't have any macro surprises.

Toggle   **Toggle**   **Turn on tuner**

Tuner here: OK I am powered up

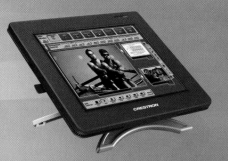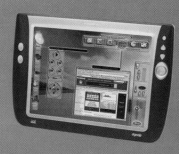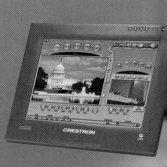

4 A professional home theater installer can provide you with a custom two-way remote system, designed specifically for the components in your personal system. In a custom system, the remote control unit is called a *system controller* and typically uses a custom-designed touch screen. At the receiving end, a *control processor* unit is connected to all your individual components; it receives the signals from the system controller, routes them to the appropriate components, and monitors feedback from the components regarding their current operating statuses.

CD jukebox: disk 1 selected: playing track 3

Now playing - CD jukebox - disk 1 - track 3
"Like A Rolling Stone" Bob Dylan
Highway 61 Revisited - 1965 (Columbia)
tap here for lyrics or karaoke

PLAYLIST
REPEAT
CONTINUOUS
RANDOM

LIGHTING / CLIMATE
AUDIO CONTROL
HOME THEATER

2 A two-way remote control receives these status commands and displays the appropriate information on its LCD screen.

Glossary

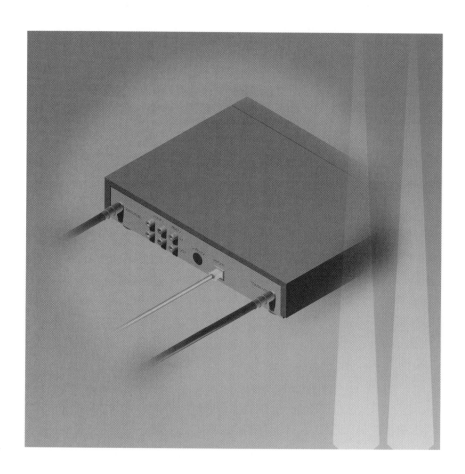

1.78:1   The shape of a wide-screen HDTV (16 × 9); this is why a small bar is present on 16 × 9 televisions when showing a wide-screen movie.

1.85:1   The most common wide-screen aspect ratio used in theatrical films.

2.35:1   The widest aspect ratio used in theatrical films today.

4:3   The NTSC standard aspect ratio for traditional TVs; a 4:3 picture is four units wide by three units high. Also measured as 1.33:1.

5.1   A surround sound system that produces five separate audio channels (front left, front center, front right, surround left, surround right) plus one subwoofer channel—thus the "5.1" designation. Both Dolby Digital and DTS are 5.1-channel systems.

6.1   A surround sound system that enhances the standard 5.1 layout with a single rear channel, located directly behind the listener.

7.1   A surround sound system that enhances the standard 5.1 layout with rear left and rear right speakers, located behind the listener.

16:9   The aspect ratio used in HDTV broadcasts; a 16:9 picture is 16 units wide by 9 units high. The 16:9 aspect ratio presents a wider image area than the traditional 4:3 ratio. Also measured as 1.78:1.

480i   The standard definition format used for traditional NTSC television broadcasts; it transmits 480 horizontal scan lines with interlaced scanning.

480p   A higher-quality variation on the standard NTSC broadcast format, transmitting 480 horizontal scan lines with progressive scanning.

720p   One of the two main HDTV formats in use today; it transmits 720 horizontal scan lines with progressive scanning.

1080i   One of the two main HDTV formats in use today; it transmits 1,080 horizontal scan lines with interlaced scanning.

1080p   An HDTV format used in some video games and future high-definition DVDs; it transmits 1,080 horizontal scan lines with progressive scanning.

A

acoustic suspension   A type of speaker enclosure that uses a sealed box to provide accurate, tight bass response.

amplifier   A component that amplifies audio signals that are then output to one or more speakers.

analog   A means of transmitting or storing data using a continuously variable signal. Prone to signal degradation, it does not always accurately reproduce the original.

anamorphic widescreen   A means of storing a wide-screen picture on a DVD so that all the horizontal scan lines are used to display the picture, with none wasted on the black bars above and below the letter-boxed picture.

aspect ratio The ratio between the width and height of a video display. The NTSC television standard is 4:3, where HDTV uses a 16:9 ratio. Some wide-screen movies use an even wider ratio, either 1.85:1 or 2.35:1.

ATSC Advanced Televisions Systems Committee, the industry group that established the new HDTV broadcast television standard. It sometimes refers to the high-definition standard itself. (An ATSC tuner is a television tuner that receives over-the-air HDTV broadcasts.)

audio/video receiver A combination of amplifier and preamplifier that controls both audio and video inputs and outputs. Also called an A/V receiver.

B–C

bandwidth Refers to the range of frequencies a component can reproduce, or the amount of information that can be carried by a circuit or signal. The larger the bandwidth, the better the sound or picture.

bass reflex A type of speaker enclosure that includes a precisely designed or "tuned" opening in the enclosure. Typically louder—though less accurate—than acoustic suspension speakers.

Blu-ray disc One of two competing high-definition DVD formats, with a storage capacity up to 50GB for a dual-layer disc.

brightness The black level of the picture.

CD Compact disc; a laser-based digital format for storing high-quality audio programming.

CD-R CD-Recordable; compact discs that can be recorded (once) by home CD recorders.

CD-RW CD-Rewritable; compact discs that can be recorded several times by computer-based CD recorders.

chrominance The color component of a video signal that includes information about the image's color (hue) and saturation.

coaxial cable A type of cable consisting of a thick copper wire surrounded by aluminum foil shielding. Traditionally used for RF transmissions, it can also be used to carry component video and digital audio signals.

coaxial digital A type of connection that transmits digital audio via a copper wire.

component video A video signal that has been split up into its component parts: red (Pr), green (Y), and blue (Pb). Component video connections—found on higher-end TVs and DVD players—reproduce the best possible picture quality, with improved color accuracy and reduced color bleeding.

composite video A single video signal that contains both chrominance (color) and luminance (brightness) and information. Composite video is typically delivered through a single "video" RCA jack connection and delivers a better-quality picture than an RF signal, but not as good as an S-Video signal.

crossover   A circuit that divides an audio signal into two or more ranges by frequency. Crossovers are typically used in a speaker system to send low-frequency signals to the woofer and high-frequency signals to the tweeter.

CRT   Cathode ray tube, commonly called a *picture tube*. Used in all direct view, all rear projection, and some front projection televisions.

D

dB   Decibel, the standard unit of measure for expressing relative power differences, otherwise known as loudness. One dB is the smallest change in loudness most people can detect; a 10 dB difference produces twice the volume.

DBS   Digital broadcast satellite, or direct broadcast satellite; the satellite broadcasting system that uses a small round or oval satellite dish to receive signals from a high-powered satellite in geosynchronous orbit.

digital   A means of transmitting or storing data using "on" and "off" bits (expressed as 1 or 0). It's known for its highly accurate reproduction, with little or no degradation from the original.

digital compression   Any algorithm that reduces the storage space required to store or transmit information. MPEG-2 and MPEG-4 are the most popular digital compression schemes in use today.

digital television   Television signals broadcast digitally. DTV comes in several formats, each with varying types of picture resolution and sound quality. The highest quality of these formats is called HDTV.

DIRECTV   One of the two main providers of digital satellite programming.

Dish Network   Owned by EchoStar, one of the two main providers of digital satellite programming.

direct view   Any video display in which the picture is produced on the viewing surface itself. Popular direct view technologies include cathode ray tube (CRT), LCD flat panel, and plasma.

DLP   Digital Light Processor, a type of microdisplay technology used in some rear projection TVs. DLP displays utilize DMDs to reproduce the final picture.

DMD   Digital micromirror device, the component in a DLP display that uses thousands of micromirrors.

Dolby AC-3   The previous name for Dolby Digital.

Dolby Digital   Surround sound format that can incorporate up to six discrete digital audio channels: front left, front center, front right, surround left, surround right, and a "low frequency effects" channel for subwoofers.

Dolby Digital EX   Extended version of the Dolby Digital surround sound format, with 6.1 channels. The extra channel is a matrixed rear surround channel positioned at the rear of the room, behind and between the left and right surrounds.

Dolby Digital Plus   New version of the Dolby Digital surround sound format designed for high-definition DVDs, offering high-bit rate performance for up to 7.1 discrete channels.

Dolby Digital TrueHD   New version of the Dolby Digital surround sound format designed for high-definition DVDs, offering lossless encoding for up to 7.1 discrete channels of 24-bit/96KHz audio.

Dolby Pro Logic   The predecessor to Dolby Digital, with only four channels: front left, front center, front right, and a single "surround" channel. The single surround channel is typically sent to two or more rear speakers. Dolby Pro Logic channels are matrixed into a left and right output, whereas Dolby Digital uses six discrete outputs.

Dolby Pro Logic IIx   A newer version of Dolby Pro Logic that, in addition to traditional Pro Logic decoding, also creates virtual surround channels from standard two-channel sources.

DSP   Digital signal processing, computer-based circuitry used in some surround sound receivers that creates different simulated sound fields.

DTS   Digital Theater Systems, a 5.1 surround sound format that competes with Dolby Digital.

DTS ES   A 6.1 version of DTS surround sound; the extra channel is a discrete rear surround positioned behind and between the left and rear surrounds.

DTS-HD   New version of the DTS surround sound format designed for high-definition DVDs, offering an unlimited number of discrete channels with lossless encoding.

DTS:Neo 6   A matrix surround sound system from Digital Theater Systems that can feed up to six speakers—front left, front center, front right, surround left, surround right, and sub-woofer. Like Dolby Pro Logic IIx, it can also create virtual surround channels from standard two-channel sources.

DTV   See *digital television.*

DVD   An audio/video laser-based disc format with storage capacities ranging from 4.7GB to 17GB.

DVD-Audio   An audio-only DVD format that delivers better-than-CD quality sound; it competes with SACD.

DVD-R   DVD-Recordable; DVD discs that can be recorded (once) by home DVD recorders. There are actually two types of DVD-recordable discs—DVD-R and DVD+R, both of which work in similar fashion but are largely incompatible with each other.

DVD-RW   DVD-Rewritable; DVD discs that can be recorded several times by home or computer-based DVD recorders. There are actually two types of DVD-rewritable discs—DVD-RW and DVD+RW, both of which work in similar fashion but are largely incompatible with each other.

DVI   Digital video interface; a type of video connection that carries the signal in pure digital format. There are three types of DVI connections—DVI-D (digital-to-digital, used in most home theater set-ups), DVI-A (digital-to-analog), and DVI-I (capable of carrying either digital-to-digital or analog-to-analog signals).

DVR   Digital video recorder, a device that records programming digitally on a large hard disk. Also known as a *personal video recorder (PVR)* or *hard disk recorder.*

dynamic range   The difference between loud and soft sounds.

E–F

EDTV   Enhanced definition television, with 480p resolution.

EPG   Electronic program guide, an onscreen listing of television, cable, or satellite programming for several days at a time.

field   When using interlaced scanning, half of a frame of picture information.

flat-panel display   One of several technologies that provides a video display on a flat, thin screen. Today's most popular flat-panel displays utilize either LCD or plasma technology.

FPTV   Front projection television, a video display device that projects a picture onto the front of a separate screen.

frame   One single still image that, when played in rapid succession with other frames, creates a moving picture.

frequency response   The range of frequencies accurately reproduced by a particular component; the wider the range, the better.

G–H

hard disk recorder   See *DVR.*

HD DVD   One of two competing high-definition DVD formats, with a storage capacity of up to 30GB for a dual-layer disc.

HDMI   An advanced form of connection that carries both audio and video signals in digital format. HDMI cables can carry up to 8 channels of digital audio, in addition to the digital video signal.

HDTV   High-definition television, a subset of the new digital TV standard that reproduces pictures in either 780p or 1080i resolution, with a 16:9 aspect ratio and Dolby Digital 5.1 surround sound.

home theater   The attempt to reproduce, as accurately as possible, the experience of watching a film in a movie theater. It typically involves a high-quality video source (such as DVD), an audio/video receiver, surround-sound speakers, and a large video display device.

home theater PC   See *Media Center PC.*

horizontal resolution   The sharpness of a video display, measured in terms of horizontal lines that can be resolved from one side of the screen to the other. Broadcast television has a horizontal resolution of 330 lines; DVDs deliver 500 lines; and HDTV can deliver up to 1,080 lines of horizontal resolution.

Hz   Hertz, a unit of measurement for the frequency of sounds. 1Hz is equal to one cycle per second, and the range of human hearing is typically 20Hz–20,000 Hz.

I–J

infrared   An area in the electromagnetic spectrum with a wavelength greater than visible light. Commonly used in handheld remote control devices.

interlaced scanning   A method of displaying television pictures in which the picture is displayed in two halves (one of odd-numbered lines, one of even-numbered lines) that are interlaced together to create the full picture.

IR   See *infrared*.

K–L

LCD display   A type of flat-panel display comprised of multiple liquid crystal display (LCD) devices.

LCD projector   A type of microdisplay device that generates a picture using a liquid crystal display, which is then projected through a magnifying lens.

LCoS   Liquid crystal on silicone; a type of microdisplay technology used in some rear projection TVs, utilizing an LCD-like component.

learning remote   A handheld remote control that can "learn" commands from other remotes.

letterbox   A method of displaying an entire wide-screen image on a narrower screen, using black bars above and below the picture.

LNB   Low noise blocker; a small amplifier located on the arm of a satellite dish that receives digital satellite transmissions.

luminance   The brightness or black-and-white component of a color video signal; determines the level of picture detail.

M

Media Center PC   A personal computer designed for home theater use, typically running the Microsoft Windows XP Media Center Edition operating system.

microdisplay   A miniature device used to generate pictures in some projection television systems. Today's microdisplay devices use DLP, LCoS, and LCD technologies.

MiniDV   Digital video recording format for camcorders that uses an ultra-small cassette.

MPEG-2   The method of compressing digital video signals used by DVDs, digital broadcast satellites, and digital and high-definition television.

MPEG-4   A newer, more efficient system of compressing video signals.

N–O

NTSC   National Television System Committee, the industry group that established the current North American analog broadcast TV standard. It sometimes refers to the standard itself.

optical digital   A type of audio connection that transmits digital signals via fiber-optic cable.

OTA   Over-the-air television broadcast signals.

P–Q

PAL   The European broadcast standard.

pan-and-scan   A technique used to display the most important parts of a wide-screen image on a narrower 4:3 ratio screen. The name comes from the panning and scanning necessary to keep the focus on the most important part of the scene, which is not always in the direct center of the picture.

PIP   Picture-in-picture, the display of a second picture in a small window within a larger picture.

pixels   The individual picture elements that make up a video image.

plasma display   A flat-panel video display that uses plasma gas to "light up" individual pixels in a picture.

POP   Picture-outside-picture, the display of a second picture in a small window outside the main picture. Typically used on wide-screen displays.

preamplifier   A component that controls or switches the various inputs from audio and video sources.

progressive scanning   A method of displaying television pictures in which the picture is displayed in a single pass, instead of the two fields used with interlaced scanning. A progressively scanned picture more accurately reproduces fast action and minimizes the visibility of flicker and scan lines.

programmable remote   A handheld remote control that can be programmed to perform multiple-component operations, typically via creating multiple-step macros. Many programmable remotes also enable the creation of custom buttons and pages on an LCD touch screen display.

PVR   Personal video recorder. See *DVR*.

R

RF   Radio frequency; any frequency within the electromagnetic spectrum associated with the propagation of radio waves (approximately 10KHz–100MHz).

receiver   A component that combines a preamplifier, an amplifier, and radio in a single chassis. Receivers that include inputs and outputs for video sources and display are called *audio/video receivers*.

resolution   The measurement of picture detail, typically measured in terms of horizontal lines that can be seen or resolved on a display. See also *horizontal resolution*.

RPTV   Rear projection television, a video display device that uses CRTs or microdisplay devices to project a picture onto the back of a translucent screen.

S

SACD   Super-audio CD; a new CD-based format that delivers better-than-CD quality sound. It competes with DVD-Audio.

scan lines   The horizontal lines, scanned one after another, that comprise the picture on a video display. (Don't confuse it with horizontal resolution, which measures the visible number of lines in a display.)

SDTV   Standard definition television; the current 480i broadcast standard.

signal-to-noise ratio   A measure of the content portion of an audio or video signal in relation to the noise contained in the signal, expressed in decibels (dB). A higher S/N ratio indicates a quieter or less noisy signal. As an example, VHS VCRs have S/N ratios in the 40 dB range, whereas DVDs have S/N ratios approaching 65 dB.

subwoofer   A speaker specially designed to reproduce a range of very low frequencies—typically 20Hz–200Hz. Subwoofers are commonly used in home theater systems to enhance the reproduction of low bass in movie soundtracks.

surround sound   The experience of being surrounded by sound from a video or an audio source. This is typically achieved with a surround sound decoder and multiple speakers.

S-VHS   Super VHS, a variation on the standard VHS format that delivers sharper pictures (400 lines of resolution versus 240 lines for standard VHS).

S-Video   A four-pin connection that transmits the chrominance (color) and luminance (brightness) portions of a video signal separately, for improved color accuracy and reduced distortion.

T

THD   Total harmonic distortion, a measurement of the noise generated by an amplifier or a receiver. The lower the number, the better.

THX   A set of high-fidelity standards, above and beyond the Dolby Digital standard, for both home theater equipment and prerecorded programming.

timeshift   The process of recording a television program for viewing at a later time.

TiVo   One of the most popular DVR services.

tweeter   A small, lightweight driver within a speaker enclosure that reproduces the highest musical frequencies.

U–V

universal remote   A single handheld remote control that contains command codes for multiple pieces of equipment and can thus operate multiple devices simultaneously.

VHS   Today's standard videocassette format.

video   Picture.

W–X–Y–Z

watt   In terms of audio equipment, a measurement of an amplifier's output power.

Wi-Fi   Wireless Fidelity; the IEEE 802.11 standard for wireless networking.

widescreen   A picture with an aspect ratio wider than 4:3 or 1.33:1.

window pane   A method of displaying a 4:3 ratio picture on a 16:9 ratio screen, using black bars on either side of the picture.

Windows XP Media Center Edition   The operating system and interface used by many Media Center or home theater PCs.

woofer   A driver within a speaker enclosure that uses a large cone to reproduce bass frequencies.

Index

HOW IT WORKS

The How It Works series offers a unique, visual, four-color approach designed to educate curious readers. From machine code to hard-drive design to wireless communication, the How It Works series offers a clear and concise approach to understanding technology—a perfect source for those who prefer to learn visually. Check out other books in this best-selling series by Que:

How Computers Work, Eighth Edition
ISBN: 0-7897-3424-9
US $29.99
CAN $44.95 UK £21.99

How Computers Work, Eighth Edition offers a unique and detailed look at the inner workings of your computer. From keyboards to virtual reality helmets, this book covers it all.

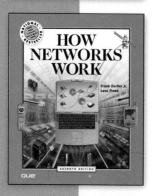

How the Internet Works, Seventh Edition
ISBN: 0-7897-2973-3
US $29.99
CAN $44.95 UK £21.99

How the Internet Works, Seventh Edition clearly explains how the Internet works and gives you behind-the-scenes information. Find out what actually happens when you send an email or purchase goods over the Web.

How Networks Work, Seventh Edition
ISBN: 0-7897-3232-7
US $29.99
CAN $44.95 UK £21.99

How Networks Work, Seventh Edition visually demonstrates how the components of a network function together, With this book, you will learn how an electric signal is transmitted, how firewalls block unwanted traffic, and how everything in between works.

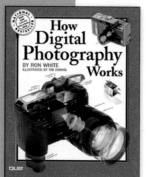

How Digital Photography Works
ISBN: 0-7897-3309-9
US $29.99
CAN $44.95 UK £21.99

How Digital Photography Works offers a behind the scenes look at digital photography. You'll understand how your digital camera captures images and how your software fixes your mistakes.

www.quepublishing.com